THE CHILDREN OF THE 'BLACK MAN'

Bishop Evans Antwi Adjei

ISBNs:
Paperback: 978-1-80227-021-1
eBook: 978-1-80227-022-8

Published by PublishingPush.com

CONTENTS

Clarification

In this book, the terms Black Man, White Man, Africans, Europeans, Slaves and Slave Masters etc. were used, not to degrade or promote any group of people, but to convey the message in the contents of this book for better understanding. The White man was at times used interchangeably with Europeans and the Black man interchangeably with Africans. The writer encourages every reader of this book to have an open mind to grasp the constructive work and purpose of this book.

About the Author

Evans Antwi-Adjei is the Leader and founder of the Golden Eagle Global Ministries, a man who believes in the power of education. He is a Motivational and a Conference Speaker and author, a man with over 25 years of experience in Leadership and a highly respected Leader in the African Community in Italy.

He has impacted many lives positively over the years through his lectures. He is bent on the idea of the importance of correctly analysing information before its application. Both in the religious and secular circles, Evans Antwi-Adjei is known for his profound wisdom, knowledge and understanding of life and human relations. His insight and understanding about the situation of the African, his challenges and the solutions to rising above his limitations are very intriguing.

The heart of Evans Antwi-Adjei is revealed in his love for humanity and his aim is for all people to live in peace. He has also dedicated himself to helping people, most especially the African (Black Man), to understand their challenges and the solutions to totally emancipate themselves and match up with the progress of the entire world.

Preface

The challenges and the issues of the Black man from the ancient past to this present age have attracted much debate. The Transatlantic slave trade, which took place some years ago, marked the Black man in a negative way because he was the main product traded. Although slavery had existed for thousands of years before that, and many people were involved in it, that of the Black man became how he was later considered among the human race.

Some Black people were taken from Africa and were sent to America and other parts of the world as slaves to work for the White man where they were maltreated and their progress hindered. At the same time, some of the Western countries colonized the African continent, subjecting the Black man to the Western system of government and using the Black people, once again, to fulfil their quest.

The Western people, also known as 'White people', introduced their education to eliminate illiteracy from the countries they colonized but their education moulded the people to simply behave like them and not to discover their own potential for self-development.

Many books and documentary films which depicted the Black man as a people of a lesser god, inferior to the White man in everything, became the conception that was crafted around the Black man. In the Motherland and abroad, the Black man was seen by every other race as a slave and his only usefulness was to serve and work for others.

The Black man's family was not considered to be a standard family because his family was just an increase to the labour force. Marriages or relationships between Black people and other people were considered as disgusting and an abnormal union because there were theories and debates that suggested that the Black man was not a human being.

Some held the belief that the Black man was a monkey; some considered him to be slightly more advanced than the monkey, whilst others assumed that he was not a human being at all because his body pigmentation was too different from the other human beings. The Black man had to put up with all these to live among human society. Those who found themselves in America had to pay a higher price daily to survive because they were forbidden and controlled by the political system. Those on the Motherland were also ruled by the White people, obeying laws and regulations set from abroad, which meant that the life of the Black man, both at home and abroad, was chaotic and subject to strict permission from their rulers whilst progress was inhibited in every way.

Nevertheless, some Black people, who saw the condition not as the majority, did everything to educate themselves to disprove the theories about the Black man by demonstrating in every sense, skills and abilities in their field of operation. More Black scholars, who graduated in various fields of studies, started to throw light on the deception around the personality of the Black man. This enlightenment reached the Motherland through some of the scholars who saw the need to return home to fight for independence to liberate the African continent from their colonial masters.

While Black scholars fought for equal rights abroad, the same fight for equal rights happened in the Motherland to bring freedom to the people. The leaders of the Black people had to pay a higher price to initiate this civil rights revolution and independence.

Their great efforts were rewarded, though most of them had to pay with their lives. Through education, hard work, determination and other principles and virtues, a new conception about the Black man was brought to light, which proved that the Black man was not an animal, neither was he inferior to any other human being, but that he was capable of ruling himself and capable of progress in everything just like every other person.

The fathers of the Black men had hoped that the Black people would understand the importance of education and self-development, hard work and the vision to develop the Motherland by uniting their forces to benefit each other. They thought that Black people would understand their struggle, appreciate their effort and implement their ideas to shatter the false conception about the Black man and raise a stronger generation of Black men who would not need to go through what they went through.

Unfortunately, this has not been the case. The situation of the Black man is disheartening. The Black man is still swimming in poverty and the Motherland is still undergoing exploitations, causing people to suffer. In the present day, Africa is ruled by Africans, but the countries are underdeveloped and infested with want and poverty. The leaders have not understood the importance of leadership as they continue to personalise the wealth of the country and fight every opposition that tries to stand against them.

Unstable governments, military controversies and unfaithful leaders have brought Africa to her knees, constantly begging for food and support. The Africans entangled by want and poverty are migrating in their numbers to the Western countries to do anything they can to survive. They run from their own brothers who rule the country and risk their lives through whatever means to enter the Western countries. Sadly, most of them refuse to work or educate themselves once they enter the West but throw themselves on social benefits and government subsidies, which is another form of mental slavery because it makes a person dependent and shaped for poverty.

In the Motherland and abroad, the Black man has not understood how vital it is for him to develop because he is still consumed by the slave-trade trauma, refusing to do anything and dwelling on accusations and rights. The Black man today is exposed to so many opportunities that his forefathers were not exposed to and had their forefathers been exposed to these opportunities, they would have changed the world. The Black man's forefathers sacrificed their lives to give a better platform to the generations to come. Sadly, the new generation does not understand the opportunity offered.

Most Black people do not know that it was education and sound moral presentations that paved the way for their fathers to obtain a good reputation. Today, bad language, accusation, lamentations, wrong concept, laziness, low self-image, bad character and attitudes have engulfed the Black man's personality.

The Black man has not understood how important it is for him to rise above all limits to affect his environment. There are other people who do worse things than the Black man, but their actions are never magnified in the same way as the Black man's negative actions simply because the success of the Black man would make some documentaries, concepts, theories, debates and so-called 'scientific' findings to be proven false. The Black man has not understood these things; instead, he keeps on worsening his own condition.

The White man can no longer be blamed for the condition of the Black man because the Black man has everything he needs to improve himself. The Black man has a mind of his own which is controlled by him; therefore, he has no excuse and simply cannot blame others for his own inability to progress. Those abroad have all the educational structures made available to them to improve themselves in every field of learning, while those in the Motherland have all the resources they need to develop themselves. The few Black people who, through education, determination, hard work and positivity, have risen above limitations, have tried to, and continue to, communicate through their conduct and achievements to all Black people that education, determination and hard work is the key.

Until the Black man understands that the White man is not the cause of his problem, he will always live in bitterness and anger, which will sabotage his potential, skills and progress. Also, such bitterness and anger can, and continues to, hinder the progress of the Black man as he continues to prove to the White man that he is capable like him. The Black man does not need to prove to the White man that he is capable. This is simply not necessary. The Black man owes himself progress, development and the ability to govern himself and to generate wealth.

Traditions and religion have contributed to the entanglement of the Black man's functionality because, in most cases, it ceases his reasoning power and renders him vulnerable to exploitation. The major factor that holds the Black man on his knees is his pattern of thought which dwells on the things that happened to him in the past.

Until the past is overcome, the future is insecure and low self-esteem, an inferiority complex and the inability to improve or upgrade oneself sets in. The past is a reservoir of information but how it is used determines whether a person rises or falls.

Treasure is in two forms, good and bad. Therefore, the accumulated wealth of a person becomes his valued treasure. When a person values anger, bitterness, hatred, accusations, lamentations, laziness, and so on, they become their valued treasure. The same is true if positive and good treasures are valued. Therefore, a person must be careful what they keep in their mind because these become the valued treasure.

A powerful leader once said that his dream was that, one day, a person would not be judged by the color of his skin but by the contents of his character. Merriam Webster dictionary defined character as the way someone thinks, feels, and behaves which indicates someone's personality. Going by this definition, until a person's character is developed, they can be a hindrance to themselves.

The easiest way to escape responsibility is to shift the blame onto others by accusing them of your condition but we must not forget that a coin always has two faces. Though the Westerners have, in some ways, been a hindrance to the Black man, the Black Man has a mind of his own and he has the right to accept or refuse anything that does not favour him. If he agrees to anything offered him, then it means that he must accept responsibility rather than shifting the blame onto someone else.

The Black man must assume responsibility for his decisions and actions, as well as the consequences. The White man is not the cause of the Black man's failure. The White man has his own problems too. The Black man is responsible for his own problems because it is about time that the Black man rose to take full control of his situation. The Black man must change the way he thinks and focus on his own potential and abilities.

Acknowledgment

I want to thank my God who has helped me in all my life, enriching me with life-changing ideas to better my life and that of others.

This book was made possible by these wonderful people who availed themselves and worked tirelessly, day and night, to support me as I wrote:

To my wife, Doris A.A. Gadson, and my children, I want to say thank you so much for believing in me, stirring and motivating me to write. You never gave up on me, but you patiently stood by me and helped me in all areas you could.

David Mawunyo Wussah, founder of Leadership Eagle which deals with Entrepreneurship and Mentorship; thank you immensely for your great contribution to getting this book printed. I cherish your work, your time and energy invested into making this book a success.

Mrs Cecelia Darko, thank you so much for believing in me and supporting me from the very first day. You are a treasure to my life and I appreciate everything you did.

Bishop Oscar Mensah, thank you for believing in me; I appreciate your advice, support and care. You stood by me when I needed your help and you covered my back when you witnessed my struggles. Thank you.

My editor, Dr Imose Itua, you patiently read over and over, considering every word, phrase and sentence, to convey the concept in this book in a more structural manner, making it readable and simple to understand. I appreciate your work and I thank you so much.

Lastly, to every reader, I appreciate you for valuing and honouring my work by purchasing a copy. May you find solutions to your questions. I wholeheartedly thank you for your kindness.

CHAPTER ONE

The Man Labelled Black

Many have been the questions, debates and controversies around the Black Man over the years. There is no group of people whose life on this earth has attracted as much attention as the Black Man. Among all the people on the face of the earth, the Black Man's body pigmentation and physical appearance differs from all other people, which has attributed to his innumerable difficulties and limitations.

A lot of evil things have been said, implemented and taught concerning the Black Man that has caused him to become a victim among all people in the world. Though this fact is denied by many, all the people who denied it have never been called Black in their lifetime; neither have they experienced for one moment the injustice the Black Man is subjected to because of his color and appearance.

Until recent times, the role of the Black Man in movies, which are a strong means of mass education, was a slave or a servant, and even when he was offered an important role, it was to defend his personality from racial attacks. The simple fact that some Black Men were taken against their will from their countries of origin and forced to become slaves in other parts of the world, has meant the Black Man has been labelled as a slave and a servant as if this was his purpose and duty on earth.

Over the years, the Black Man has proved, in many ways, his equal ability in all arenas of life, but no matter what he does, it is already registered in the minds of people that he is inferior and less important among the human race.

In the religious circle, some have taught that the Black Man is the descendant of Cain who was cursed by God for killing his brother. Some say the Black Man is not a pure human being, whilst some even hold the fact that he is not a human being at all. Such labelling has affected the Black Man immensely within his family life, social life, economic life and even his academic life. Whether in the Motherland, which is the African Continent, or in any other place where the Black Man dwells, life has not been easy. The negative conception and descriptions of him have preceded him making it difficult for him to live peacefully and successfully.

The Black Man has had to defend a name that he did not give to himself, making him lose his original identity because he is busy trying to disprove the negative image given him through the adjective 'Black' qualifying him as a Man.

The Bible is a book that explains the creation and the origin of Man. According to the writings of Moses in the book of **Genesis, Chapter 1 and verses 26 – 28**, God, the Supreme being, made Man after His image and likeness, Male and Female and He blessed them. There is nowhere written in the Bible that God created a Black or White, Blue or Red, Yellow or Green Man. God simply created man.

The pigmentation of Man's body wasn't an issue because all that mattered was that he was created in the image of his maker. It is very clear that God did not divide Man into different categories or races. The division was the perfect work of Man himself to set up a system of superior and inferior humans, first-class and second-class humans, masters and slaves, to open doors for exploitation, dictatorship, control, power, racism, war and many more. Superior man had the right to do whatever he liked whenever he wanted because he classified himself as the pure and correct human, whereas the inferior man needed the permission of the superior man to live.

Division, classification and qualification among men became a necessity. The African was labelled Black because of his color and a slave or servant because of what was taught about his personality. Over time, many negative meanings have been attached to the words 'Black man' and this has, and will continue, to haunt him and deprive the African from knowing his true identity. Remember that 'The African' did not call himself Black but had to accept and adapt to the limitations and humiliations, the insult and disrespect the word Black carries.

Merriam Webster Dictionary defines Black as follows;

"People who have dark skin and who come originally from Africa. It must be acknowledged that:

Black also refers to dirty

Black means absence of light

Black means thoroughly sinister or evil

Black means wicked

Black is indicative of condemnation or discredit

Black connects with or invokes the supernatural, especially the Devil

Black means very sad, gloomy or calamitous

Black is also characterized by hostility or anger

Black is characterized as grim, which means unpleasant or shocking to see or think about

Black means grotesque, which means a style of art characterized by fanciful or fantastic human and animal forms often interwoven with foliage or similar figures that may distort the natural into absurdity, ugliness or caricature monsters.

Black means satire, which means a way of using humour to show that someone or something is foolish, weak, bad etc., humour that shows the weakness or bad qualities of a person, government, society etc..."

With these definitions associated with the word 'Black', it is evident why the man labelled Black is not respected among all people, because there is nothing positive seen to come out of him. To many, he is more or less a monster, a creative mistake or a case to study.

Whenever the term Black People or Black zone is mentioned, the following are greatly expected:

Crime, Poverty, Sickness, Dirtiness, Disorder, Anger/Rage, Low Mentality, Drugs, Violence/Harshness, Illiteracy, Human-animals, Monsters, Ugly and Strange things, Bizarre, Unusual, Abnormality, Incapability, Superficial, Unserious, Beggars and Lawlessness.

These things are expected to be seen wherever a Black Man dwells. Most times, because these are the things the Black Man has been painted with, his presence in any neighbourhood becomes very suspicious. The Black Man has had to put up with these things daily because the adjective that qualifies his personality, classifies him as a monstrous individual.

Until he realises that he is not as he is painted, and he stops adapting to the negative words that surround his personality, the progress of the Man labelled 'Black' will continue to remain a struggle.

Most great leaders of the Black People, such as Martin Luther King Jnr, Dr Kwame Nkrumah, Nelson Mandela, Thomas Sankara and many more, understood the deception around the Black Man and started to tell them that there is nothing wrong with them and that they were capable of doing what everyone else was doing. Most of the fathers of the Black Man paid the price with their lives to educate them about the truth concerning their personality. They did that gladly hoping that, one day, their children would bring about positive changes which would eradicate the falsehoods that had been spread about the Man Labelled 'Black'.

"Who is a Black man?"

CHAPTER TWO

The Fathers/The Leaders

Fathers and leaders are very important to every society because they are the visionaries and they lay down the right foundations to build the family, community or the nation. Every country is built by leaders who are visionaries, who see the state of their people and strategize structures that will develop the country. Leaders also set up institutions that boost the morals and the abilities of the people.

The fathers of the Western countries took their time to help their people. They fought battles and conquered territories and enslaved people to build up their lives. They built their countries with well-planned structures to favour their people for generations to come. The blueprint of their work was designed in such a way that it gave room for the progressive developments which we see today. They preserved the legacies of their fathers and taught about them as if they were infallible. They made sure their fathers were perceived and respected as supreme, powerful and incomparable.

Unlike them, the fathers of the Africans were enslaved, imprisoned and killed before they could teach what they discovered. The Africans were forced to hate their fathers and see them as liars and failures. The rich stories about some of the African leaders that could have ignited a positive image and pride in the Africans were hidden and never allowed to be taught and anything made in Africa became a byword for inferior quality, whether it concerned the people or their finished product. The few fathers of the Africans who stood for their people had to pay a huge price to pave the way for their development. In almost all the cases, they were overthrown or killed.

When the visionary is killed, progress and development are halted and compromised; the people, therefore, fall into the tentacles of poverty which causes them to be underdeveloped. It is not everyone who has the wisdom, vision or plan to build a country. The fathers whom we call leaders, who have good hearts and good conscience towards the people, use the country's resources, whether in the form of people concerning knowledge and skills, or material things as well as agricultural resources, and they administer them to the betterment of the people. There is no nation or people who can develop without good leaders, because good leaders are the pivots of a society. Until good leaders are received and allowed to lead, the whole nation remains stagnant and vulnerable, opening doors for exploitation.

The African continent is one continent that has been exploited to date. Though the continent is rich in all kinds of resources in both people and minerals, its people remain the poorest on the face of the earth because of bad leadership. Leaders who do not have the people or the nation at heart ascend to power and exploit their own people. They allow outsiders to extract all the wealth of their countries, both human and material resources, leaving the country in debt, want and suffering. Unfortunately for Africa, through ignorance, many good leaders were prevented by the same Africans from helping the people, and outsiders, who knew the importance of Africa's development, took advantage.

As explained in the next chapter, there were 'a few good men' who tried to raise Africa from the regressed state to a comparable standard with other non-African countries, but they could not complete their work. Some were killed whilst others met challenges that hindered any progress.

"The Black man exploits his people"

A Life Lived is a Life Shared

On September 21st 1909, Dr Kwame Nkrumah the Great was born to the people of Africa and, precisely, to the nation of Ghana. He left Ghana to advance his studies in the United States of America in 1935 and, after obtaining many degrees in different fields of education, he returned to Ghana, then known as Gold Coast, in 1947, which was under the colonial rule of the British.

Dr Kwame Nkrumah and his mates led Gold Coast out of the colonial rule and won independence for the nation on the 6th of March 1957 and the country became known as Ghana. He then became the Prime Minister and later the first President of Ghana and started to develop the nation. Dr Kwame Nkrumah said in his speech, on the day of independence,

"The independence of Ghana is meaningless unless it is linked up to the total liberation of the African continent".

This statement won him the honour as one of the fathers of Africa, a man who had a great vision for his people, not only for his country of origin but also the entire continent of Africa.

Dr Kwame Nkrumah's heart for his people was so big and profound that he started developing Ghana and helping other African nations to obtain independence. He saw the need for Africa to unite their forces to help their development. His vision was too big for the African leaders of his time, let alone his country of origin.

The Western countries knew that his vision was the solution Africa needed but his people were not ready for that change. In as much as he tried to convince his people to trust him, they hated him and rebelled against his administration. They overthrew him from power with the help of foreign support and handed over Ghana to military rule. Many believe that this was fuelled by some world super-powers.

Little did the Ghanaians know that the vision for their development was stopped and the room for exploitation was re-opened. His people did not know that Dr Kwame Nkrumah's ideas were a threat to the foreign beneficiaries to cut the exploitation of Ghana and Africa as a whole. When he ignited the idea of African unity, Europe was represented by individual countries. Though they were developed as individual nations, after many years, they have implemented the same idea that Dr Kwame Nkrumah suggested to the African leaders. Today, Europe has united and are benefitting from each other, but Africa remains divided and is still struggling with her many resources.

Dr Kwame Nkrumah was painted as a dictator, a monster and a wicked leader by his people and the outside world because he told Africa to unite and Ghana to help in this unification. For this reason, his people hated him and rejected his ideas. They burnt his books and broke his statues. Painful debates about his leadership strategies arose and that scared the future generation from following in his footsteps.

Until recent years, Ghana chose military rule which contributed to the stagnancy and suffering of the people. Dr Kwame Nkrumah died in exile on 27th of April 1972, because his own people rejected him and considered his ideas oppressive.

In the year 2000, Dr Kwame Nkrumah was voted Africa's Man of The Millennium by listeners to the BBC World Service. He was described by the BBC as a Hero of Independence and an international symbol of freedom as the leader of the first African country to shake off the chains of colonial rule.

In September 2009, the late President of Ghana, John Atta Mills, declared 21st September, which was the 100th anniversary of Dr Kwame Nkrumah's birth, to be **Founders' Day**, a statutory holiday in Ghana to celebrate the legacy of Dr Kwame Nkrumah.

How can a man who was dishonoured and humiliated, a man whose ideas were abhorred, a man who was painted as a monster, be voted years later as the Man of The Millennium, a Hero, and now be recognized as the Founder of Ghana by the same nation and people that rejected and overthrew him?

As a Leader, the Ghanaians never knew his value; they never understood how vital it was for them that he paved the way for their development. He saw something that the majority could not see, and he warned his people, but no one listened; neither was he given the chance to demonstrate his vision. Instead, he was rejected. The little development he encouraged in his days remains an iconic treasure to the people of Ghana.

Dr Kwame Nkrumah left the blueprint for the work he was not allowed to complete but who would listen and upgrade those ideas? Those ideas need to be upgraded and developed and this will create more value than the celebration created by staying away from work. The greatest way to celebrate a leader is to implement and upgrade his ideas but not to have a relaxing holiday in his memory where most of the people do not even know the reason for the celebration.

In one of his final speeches, Dr Kwame Nkrumah said,

"As far as I am concerned, I am in the knowledge that death cannot extinguish the torch which I have lit in Ghana and Africa. Long after I am dead and gone, the light will continue to burn and be borne aloft, giving light and guidance to all people".

In 1997, the former President of Tanzania, Julius Kambarage Nyerere said, in his speech as he visited Accra-Ghana, that,

"There were occasional instances where I debated with Kwame Nkrumah. I told him his idea of African Unity was not going to work because he was doing it for propaganda purposes. Long after his overthrow and subsequent death, it took me ten years of consistent study to get the full import of what he was talking about. In fact, Kwame Nkrumah is the greatest African ever".

Bob Marley said in his Redemption song,

"How long shall they kill our Prophets while we stand aside and look?"

Africans still do not understand the value of leaders and most of the leaders do not understand the value of leadership. In the tender stage of Africa, the fathers were not allowed to attend to the proper growth and development of Africa to craft the needed blueprint. Now, she has grown, and her mentality is well-framed, therefore, change has become difficult though the problems are evident. Africans did not only stand aside and watch; rather, they contributed to the killing of their Leaders/prophets and now they lament the foreign exploitation.

Dr Kwame Nkrumah had a foresight and started to draw the attention of his people to his foresight, but the people could not see; neither could they understand the times and the seasons. A great leader was given to Africans to pave the way to their freedom and development, to lay the foundation for unification but the people rejected him and chose the way of permanent physical and mental slavery.

Africa can never forget this great leader though his assignment was shortened and his ideas misunderstood. His words were so true and his predictions were excellent. No matter what was said about him to obscure his ideas and works, the condition of Africa has proved him right and has proved him to be a great leader. The denial of some people of his good intentions for his country has been beaten because his works still stand unchallenged and his prototype is still to be found. He stands unique and undisputable as Dr Kwame Nkrumah the Great.

"The Black man seeks for unity and Independence"

I Have a Dream

It was not the European American alone who worked and sacrificed their lives for the land but the African American also contributed through his limited resources to ensure that their new found home became a better place for all.

The European American considered himself the master while he classified the African American as a 'slave', a word that marked the African American and caused him to be unwanted in the land. The African American was denied the right to participate in the nation's affairs and was highly discriminated against in all sectors. The African American's life was made miserable in the land of promise, a land where both the European American and the African American found themselves living together.

The European American, who classified himself as White man, made life so difficult and unbearable for the African American, whom he labelled as Black. The conflict moved from two American groups into a war between White and Black. Unfortunately for the Black man, the political power was in the hands of the White man who passed strict measures and shameful laws to degrade the personality and the potential of the Black man.

The few Black men who tried to stand up and expose the hypocrisy in the land attracted the political powers against them, because most of them had no political role in the nation, so their actions were considered improper and most of them were arrested, some were threatened with beatings and some were even killed. Life was so miserable for the Black man to the extent that he had to give up his seat on the public bus for the White man to sit, though he had paid for his own ticket. The Black man could not use the same public toilets or restaurants as the White man, or anything that was of public use because it was considered a crime which was punishable by law.

Though the land was vast enough to contain and feed all the people, racism and injustice continued to divide them. The White man was assumed to be the best, the one who can do all things, perfect in his ways and a superior human being, whereas the same White man attacked and ensnared the Black man by political control, taking away his right to improve himself. The Black man was depicted as a slave, a parasite, a burden, a waste to get rid of and a race to keep under strict control. This gave permission for White citizens to brutalise the Black citizens any way they wanted because the law was bent on their side, which was an abuse of the democratic standards of the nation.

The only way the Blacks could respond to these injustices was to mobilize themselves and demonstrate on the streets to attract the attention of the government, but it always turned out to be more of a brutal experience than what they already bore. This beautiful nation, which was known as a super-power to the outside world, a dreamland for many adventurous people, a democratic exemplary to nations and a deliverer to the weaker nations in the world, faced a severe identity crisis. The White men could not relate to their fellow brothers on the land because they saw them as slaves, and the racist venom kept on devouring the nation creating permanent damage in the minds of its citizens.

Hatred between White and Black men became inevitable. The country's future was endangered by people who only saw and thought of their own generation and their present control of affairs. The purpose of life was compromised, and the thirst for power and racial superiority was the goal, until a man who saw things differently appeared on the scene.

From a distance, Martin Luther King saw the injustice that covered the land of promise, a land that was big enough to satisfy everyone, yet some of the people were denied the right to live happily.

Dr Martin Luther King Jr., born on the 15th of January 1929, a young handsome preacher of the gospel of Christ, emerged in his late twenties and saw that the great eagle was turning into a vulture, taking pleasure in eating dead meat instead of fresh meat. He saw that if nothing was done about the condition of the United States of America, the racial hatred would reach its peak, breaking down the nation.

Dr Martin Luther King Jr. was a Black man, from the side of the citizens who were denied the right to function and enjoy equally the benefits of the country. He loved his country and the people who lived in it, but he disliked the injustice the Black people suffered.

As a preacher, he knew what the Bible said concerning loving one another and living in peace, benefitting from one another, and yet, his country practised the opposite. He lifted his voice against injustice and spoke on behalf of the afflicted. He pinpointed to the authorities their favouritism and racial contour lines which promoted hatred among the people.

Though he received many threats, he never allowed anyone to intimidate him. His speeches were so powerful that it made many White people realise the twisted life of America. He risked his life as a young man knowing the consequences of his bold stand. He knew which group of Americans held the political power and he persuaded them to look into the future by putting an end to the horrible injustice other Americans like him suffered.

He stood with the people against the bus boycott, where the Black men refused to board the public bus because they were harassed by the White men to give up their seats. Many Black people who refused to give up their seat were attacked by the White men and the law. Dr King had his house bombed and he was arrested 29 times in his stand for civil rights.

On the 28th of August 1963, Dr Martin Luther King Jr. and his colleagues organized a non-violent march for jobs and freedom, an end to racial segregation in public schools, meaningful civil rights' legislation, including a law prohibiting discrimination in employment, protection of civil rights workers from police brutality, a 2-dollar minimum wage for all workers and a self-government for Washington DC. Over 250,000 people attended as Dr Martin Luther King Jr. delivered the dream for the United States of America which was to be the expected lifestyle of every American citizen. In his 17-minute speech, the statements below became the hope for all Americans:

"I say to you today, my friends, so even though we face the difficulties of today and tomorrow, I still have a dream. It is a dream deeply rooted in the American dream"

"I have a dream that one day, this nation will rise up and live out the true meaning of its creed; we hold these truths to be self-evident, that all men are created equal"

"I have a dream that one day, on the red hills of Georgia, the sons of former slaves and the sons of former slave owners would be able to sit down together at the table of brotherhood"

"I have a dream that one day, even the state of Mississippi, a state sweltering with the heat of injustice, sweltering with the heat of oppression, would be transformed into an oasis of freedom and justice"

"I have a dream that one day, my four little children will live in a nation where they will not be judged by the color of their skin but by the content of their character"

"I have a dream that one day, down in Alabama, with its vicious racists, with its governor having his lips dripping with words of interposition and nullification, one day, right there in Alabama, little Black boys and Black girls will be able to join hands with little White boys and White girls as sisters and brothers"

"I have a dream".

On April 3rd of 1968, Dr Martin Luther King Jr. delivered a speech at the Mason Temple, the world headquarters of the Church of God in Christ. His flight to Memphis had been delayed because of a bomb threat. Therefore, he and his entourage checked in at the Lorraine Motel in Memphis Abernathy. In his speech at the Mason Temple, Dr Martin Luther King Jr. said:

"And then I got to Memphis. And some began to say the threats or talk about the threats that were out. What would happen to me from some of our sick White brothers? Well, I don't know what will happen now. We've got some difficult days ahead now. But it

doesn't matter with me now. Because I have been to the mountain top. And I don't mind. Like anybody, I would like to live a long life. Longevity has its place. But I'm not concerned about that now. I just want to do God's will. And He's allowed me to go up to the mountain. And I've looked over. And I've seen the promise land. I may not get there with you. But I want you to know tonight, that we, as a people, will get to the promise land. So, I'm happy tonight. I'm not worried about anything. I'm not fearing any man. My eyes have seen the glory of the coming of the Lord".

On the 4th of April 1968, Dr Martin Luther King Jr. was shot dead as he stood on the balcony of the motel at the age of 39 years. He saw the future of America and he declared it and he stood and spoke boldly, drawing the attention of the authorities to their solemn duties. He gave hope to the hopeless and gave a dream to the citizens of America on how they must live. Though he lived a very short life, the impact he made on the United States of America opened the eyes of the citizens to change their way of thinking.

Without controversy, Dr Martin Luther King Jr. is one of the greatest leaders the United States of America has ever produced and a true leadership model to the entire world. Many negative things were spoken about him to sabotage his great work towards the injustice of his people and many other American citizens. After his death, things started to change in America and a lot has been improved towards fulfilling the American dream.

"The Black man dreams, is hopeful and fearless and ready to die to see justice served"

Cry Freedom

The downfall of a man is not the end of his life. How could he watch a nation that was rich and had an abundance to feed everybody be controlled wickedly by just one group of people? The situation was not just bad but evil. The abuse of power was evident both within and outside the country. People demonstrated on the streets to abolish apartheid. The racial venom that almost destroyed the United States of America was put on open display in South Africa. The political powers in South Africa made their intentions very clear that, as White people, they wanted every other person with different pigmentation to be separated from them. They denied all other people the same benefits that they had in the same country.

Such behaviour depicted a very negative image of who the White man was and their intentions concerning other people who did not look like them was frowned upon. Life for all other people, and most especially the Black man on the land, was horrible. The political power of the nation which was in the hands of the White man was so badly abused that the whole world witnessed what was meant by 'White power'.

Just like what happened in the United States of America, it was clearly signposted where Blacks could go and where they could not go. Black people could not cross the racial contour lines. Likewise, all non-White citizens had their limitations. As usual, the political powers made sure that no political party was permitted to disturb the racial benefits achieved through segregation. Any leader of any permitted political party was closely monitored, most times banned from public appearances or imprisoned through false accusation for attempting to overthrow the present government. The wealth and the beauty of South Africa were channelled to the enjoyment of the White man who saw himself as pure and superior to any other person living in the country.

Many people arose and started to draw attention to the injustice and perverse leadership format that governed the country. Most were arrested and jailed, while some were brutally killed, but the more they were killed the more was the 'cry for freedom'; freedom from apartheid, freedom from injustice, freedom from wicked leadership and freedom from improper division of the country's wealth and resources.

Nelson Mandela became the hope for the afflicted citizens and the world. He became the rightful candidate to accomplish the great task to ensure justice was served for the Black man. Nelson Mandela, born on the 18th of July 1918, saw the oppression and the injustice that ruled South Africa. He dedicated his life to fighting against apartheid and for human rights. He and his colleagues took up the challenge, appealing to the South African government to end apartheid by abolishing the inhumane laws that oppressed the Black man and any man of color. His fight was for a 'free people' and to build a nation that gave equal opportunities to all citizens. His name became very popular as he was respected as the Messiah of South Africa.

In 1952, the South African government banned him from public appearance and restricted him to speaking to only one person at a time. This forced him to go underground. The man who stood boldly for his people, bringing hope for a change, was quietened and banned from public places. However, that did not stop Nelson Mandela. He went on, with his colleagues, to fight for the freedom of South Africa.

Nelson Mandela was arrested in July 1962 and, alongside his colleagues, accused of sabotage, treason and violent conspiracy. Nelson Mandela and seven other defendants narrowly escaped the gallows and were instead sentenced to life imprisonment during the so-called Rivonia Trial, a case that lasted for eight months and attracted substantial international attention. In a stirring opening statement that sealed his ionic status around the world, Nelson Mandela boldly denounced the injustice of apartheid and openly declared these words and was prepared for any decision attained by the court:

"I have cherished the ideal of a democratic and free society in which all persons live together in harmony and with equal opportunities. It is an ideal I hope to live for and to achieve. But if need be, it is an ideal for which I am prepared to die".

On 12th June 1964, when Nelson Mandela was sentenced to life imprisonment, he was 45years old. He accepted the challenge to live or to die for what he believed. The South African government continued to soak itself in higher levels of injustice and killings to nourish the apartheid ideology. The international press became aware of the injustices in South Africa and revealed the state of the people to the outside world.

At this time, a young dynamic leader of the Black people, by the name of **Steve Biko,** was unjustly brutalised and killed for his stand against apartheid. His death threw more light on the state of affairs in South Africa. The international attention grew stronger and the cry for freedom became heard.

On the 11th of February 1990, Nelson Mandela was released from prison. Then, he was 71 years old. He and many others paid dearly for a true democratic South Africa and, as he had said, it was an ideal for which he was prepared to die. Nelson Mandela did not die as was expected by his accusers, but he lived to fulfil the ideal he believed in.

In 1994, Nelson Mandela became the first Black President of South Africa. He encouraged forgiveness and promoted reconciliation by setting up a multiracial government of national unity and proclaimed the country a rainbow nation at peace with itself and the world. He lived as an example to the world and a mentor to many leaders by demonstrating what was meant by true democracy.

Nelson Mandela was a legend, a man who did not allow his pain to cause him to take revenge against his enemies. Rather, he demonstrated the qualities of a great leader by showing South Africa and the world how a country ought to be governed.

"The Black man is just, persistent and
perseveres through hardship"

The Upright Man

The time at his disposal was very limited but there were so many things to do. The political power before him did not address the needs of the people. The people depended upon their colonial masters and the land was dry and impoverished. Though there was a head of state, they were not free to operate on their own without the permission of their colonial masters. The wealth of the country was shifted and managed by only a few people. Upper Volta, as the country was known, did not make any impact except for the few who benefited from the country's resources and system of government.

On the 4th of August 1983, Thomas Sankara became the President of Upper Volta. He was just 33 years of age. As a military man who ascended to the seat of government, he knew that anything could happen though he had a lot of things to do. He did not waste time but immediately made his plans and intentions known, which was not favored by the colonial masters.

He changed the country's colonial name from Upper Volta to Burkina Faso which means **the Land of the Upright Man**. This was a message sent across the country to alert everyone to the change that had been initiated. He immediately launched one of the most ambitious programs for social and economic change ever attempted on the continent of Africa. He clearly made it known to his people and the world that Burkina Faso was not going to depend on foreign aid but would roll up its sleeves and work as any country that wanted to develop.

He knew that his decision would be met by resistance and that his people may not welcome the decision to reject foreign aid since his people were already used to having foreign aid. As no previous leader in Burkina Faso had ever attempted what he proposed, he knew that he needed to champion the course. He laid down his international and domestic policies, something which was very strategic.

Some of his domestic policies were focused on preventing famine through agrarian self-sufficiency and land reforms. Some of his policies included: prioritizing education with a nationwide literacy campaign, and promoting public health by vaccinating 2.5 million children against meningitis, yellow fever and measles etc. One of his major plans included the planting of 10 million trees to stop the growing desertification of the **Sahel**. He encouraged every village to build their own medical dispensary.

350 communities built their own schools themselves in support of his educational campaign. His commitment to women's rights caused him to outlaw female genital mutilation, forced marriages and polygamy.

Thomas Sankara wanted all Africans to know that if laziness could be eliminated by stopping the dependence on foreign aid, and hard work could be implemented through economic self-sufficiency, poverty and hunger would be eradicated from the continent. As much as he tried to invite the participation and collaboration of his people to fuel his ideas and vision for the country, he was considered a dictator. Most Africans are not used to self-discipline or hard work. They hope for their needs to be supplied. Therefore, anything that demands their temporal sacrifice to better their future becomes oppressive. They prefer enforced hard work where they gain nothing except their daily bread.

Thomas Sankara promoted the building of railway lines to connect the entire country to facilitate movement. Most of his policies were not entirely welcomed by some of the people because it involved them giving up too much to promote the development of their country. Nevertheless, he was still able to help his people and paved a notable way for future development.

On the 15th of October 1987, Thomas Sankara was brutally assassinated by his own people. Surprisingly, his successor stood against all his policies and turned the nation back to foreign aid. He affirmed by his actions that Burkina Faso could not survive without being aided.

Thomas Sankara, just like most great African leaders, was ignorantly misunderstood by his people. Though he lived only a short time, he had a lot in his heart for his people. He found a sustainable solution to help his people and instill the method of self-development and discipline, but time and a people that were not ready to sacrifice for change destroyed him. In killing Thomas Sankara, Burkina Faso eliminated a masterpiece that was pre-ordained to construct their way to total emancipation. Africa lost a great leader who believed in the abilities of his people, that if they were genuinely guided and motivated, they could do anything.

"The Black man suffers indiscipline/impatience and is hasty to make his daily bread"

CHAPTER THREE

The Father's Struggle

A good father goes the extra mile to lay the right foundation on which his children can develop. At the back of his mind, he believes that his children will value his struggles, pains, and his blood, shared to bring them freedom. The joy of a father is to see his children become more successful than what he achieved by improving or working hard on the blueprint laid down to make life easier for them.

In the automobile companies, vehicles are highly improved today to make them better and more comfortable for human use compared with those that were made 60 years ago. The inventors who crafted the first ideas of vehicles would be very proud to see what their children have done today because of the immense improvement they have brought to the automobile industries. If after 60 or 70 years, the automobile company was still struggling over how to make a vehicle run 100 kilometers per hour, and how to improve the comfortability of its passengers, then the early inventors would be highly disappointed. It would mean that little or no effort had been made to improve the knowledge. Taken another way, it would imply that no value was placed on the discovered invention. It also suggests that the struggles and sacrifices and blood shared to invent and conserve the knowledge was not cherished.

Every leader's vision in standing for a right or fighting for a people or in discovering a truth is to see the children making good use of their effort by improving on it and passing on the values of development to the next generation. It is true that the most disappointing moment for a leader is to see that what he stood for and fought for was not valued and improved on, but rather destroyed and abandoned.

The development achieved by many companies, businesses, countries, and families has brought great joy to the founding fathers, whether alive or passed. Some countries fought great wars to defend and conquer more territories to build the future for their people. After many years, their children have made good use of the freedom won for them and have developed their countries and improved the standard of living of the citizens, which is an indication that they valued and cherished the sacrifice of their fathers.

Due to the colonial rule that governed Africa for years, it took great effort and sacrifices to obtain independence for the nations. A lot of blood was shed for this cause. The founding fathers bargained their way through complex colonial systems to prove that the Black man was capable of ruling his own people.

The founding fathers of the colonial liberation saw greatness in the people of Africa and the ability to do their own things like their colonial masters if Africa could operate without interference. Though they knew of the troubles and the difficulties that could arise, they believed in progressive development with hard work. They hoped that their people would understand the importance of making their homeland comfortable by investing their abilities and skills to develop the nations.

The risk they took to undergo torture and pain reflected their strong conviction that their people were ready to live a life of dignity and integrity. They saw a better future for their people due to their response for freedom and from foreign exploitation. They believed that their people were ready for a change, either radical or progressive.

They saw the joy of a free soul, the excellency of equal opportunities, the power of freedom of speech and the integrity of social acceptance as they fought for independence and for human rights. The fathers stood against imperialism and tribalism to unite the people under one constitution. They made their voices and intentions very clear through their selfless life examples.

Most of them died without wealth, except the wealth embedded in the legacy that they left behind. They jeopardized the life of their own families to pave the way for an entire people. Under no circumstances should these great leaders' effort be undermined or forgotten because they struggled and fought for good causes and they hoped with great conviction for a better future for their people.

Does the state of African countries today and the lives of Black people in general truly reflect the value of their fathers' struggles? How best have the Black people utilized the freedom won for them and what development have they brought based on what they inherited?

"Sacrifices made; were these appreciated/valued?"

CHAPTER FOUR

The Burden of Freedom

The cry of the oppressed, afflicted or enslaved person is to be free. The worst kind of life is having to live under another person's command, to obtain permission to speak, act and do anything. For many years, this was how a lot of people lived their lives. They were not permitted by another to think and do anything by themselves. Many people were, and are still, living in great fear because another human being has taken their rights either through religious, economic or political power; they are forced to think and function according to the desired system of their oppressors.

Oppressors are people who take pleasure in afflicting others forcefully to do what they desire by imposing their authority, power and supremacy. An oppressor can be someone from another country who sees himself as superior or someone within the same country who thinks he is better than the rest and has the right to afflict others because he thinks that he knows everything.

The people who are free in this world are very few, though most people claim to be free. The people who control the world and decide how people must live are also very few. That is why, before a person can do anything, they have to go through a lot of processes to obtain permission from someone who is superior and sometimes opportunities could be denied them because somebody did not like the idea. Somebody decides what is good or bad for the society, and what is acceptable or unacceptable.

The food we eat, the dress we wear, the car we drive, the house we buy, and practically everything we want are all controlled by someone or a few people who determine how, when and where to get them. There are certain things that are forbidden for some people to have though they might have the money to buy them because someone decides who must have them.

This is a system which can be taken as the norm. However, the oppression of some people is beyond human imagination. In some countries, some women are not permitted to expose their faces publicly because someone does not like it and some women are not permitted to go to school because someone decides what is good for women. The sad thing is that the person who makes the decision is not even a woman and can never understand the woman.

The oppression that Black people have gone through and are still suffering now is both afflicted and self-made. Afflicted, because most of the Black man's assaults are connected to his color, self-made for the conclusions highlighted above, which displayed the Black man as lacking the ability and opportunities to free himself from slavery and bondage. The color of the Black man has won him several degrading medals because the one who arrested some Black people, and took them against their will at gun point to a far country, called them 'slaves', and oppressed them painfully with documented fact. Sadly, this is being taught and studied at school. This has left serious degrading marks on the personality of the Black man.

This cruel act has affected the Black man, because wherever he is found, the first thing that enters the mind of people around him is that 'he is a slave', and he is inferior, without giving him an opportunity to express or demonstrate his ability.

Many employers turn the application for employment down when they find out that the applicant is a Black man, no matter his qualification, because it is registered in the subconscious mind of people who are sometimes employers that the Black man is a slave. Most employers do not want to associate with the Black man because they perceive it as degrading to their personalities, thus, employing a Black man would affect the credibility of their organization.

Though slavery was abolished many years ago in the Western countries and human right laws were set in place, the struggle of the

Black man is buried deep within the subconscious mind of many people. Therefore, though the Black man has obtained his freedom by law and on paper, the law cannot tell people what and how to think. This is reflected in the attitudes and reactions towards the Black man. This simply suggests that the war that was won was only won in writing in many places but not truly in practice. The war, therefore, continues.

The fight for true freedom continues. This time, however, it is more psychological and political than physical. The government cannot force people to love one another. Due to the wrong images created over the years that have degraded the personality of the Black man, the limitation placed on the Black man can be mitigated. Therefore, if the government would encourage full liberation of the Black man by providing correct education to the people concerning the Black man and making them aware of the injustice that was served him, this may serve as a major step to eradicating the misinformation passed on from generations about the Black man.

Education is the key; anything that has been programmed can be unprogrammed and anything that has been written wrongly can be rewritten correctly. The Black people, the White man and the entire world at large have a lot to learn to improve the relationship between humanity. Much information about humans has been twisted to promote hatred and wickedness among men. Humans take advantage, one of another, killing themselves to prove their superiority and making the world difficult and dangerous to live in. Instead of a generation making things easier for the next, weapons of mass destruction are being prepared for destruction of the human race.

Lovely little children grow up to become permanent enemies, segregated by color and race as if there are different human races on this earth. The joy and the benefits that should be derived from the mutual relationship of humans have been turned to hatred and war, killings and oppression.

Freedom has its own burden. Consider the following narrative: whenever a person is under oppression or afflicted, the oppressor does the thinking whiles the oppressed does the work. The oppressed does not contribute in anything except his forced labor. The oppressor plans everything and calculates all his benefits. He is not obligated to teach his slave anything because he does not consider him as a family member, but rather, as his tool or equipment. If he teaches the oppressed anything, it is just to make him become more efficient in his labor.

The oppressed sees the oppressor enjoying his labor and making more money and wealth while he sinks in poverty. He begs for food and he eats measured meals just to sustain him for the next day's work, whereas the oppressor's dogs eat abundantly from the many leftovers.

These awful conditions cause the oppressed to desire freedom. He speaks about his state and plans to escape or fight for his liberation. After many attempts, freedom comes his way. He eats and drinks to his satisfaction and sleeps all day to recover from the hard work. He engages in singing and dancing and making merry until he wakes up one day and realizes that his source of supply is diminished or, at worst, finished and his oppressor is also gone.

Now he must look for a way to survive which may involve either going to look for his oppressor and begging for food by willfully surrendering his rights of freedom, or he steals from his people and runs away, or he takes responsibility to work hard more than when he did under oppression to establish himself.

The oppressed never calculates that freedom has its own burden. He never considers that it takes discipline and hard work to put food on the table. It takes thinking to know what to plant at a given season, and it takes careful calculation to know how to sell and make a profit. The oppressed only sees his affliction and his lack, but he fails to consider that, to obtain freedom, a person must be ready to assume great responsibility.

Liken this to the following scenario: A 16-year-old boy claims to be a man and, therefore, rejects his parents' order and discipline, refuses to abide by the rules of the home, fights for his freedom, but fails to calculate that as soon as he moves from his parents' house, he must rent his own house, pay his own rent and bills and buy his own food. He fails to consider that he has to think and plan his own future to prove to his parents that he is capable of catering for himself. If he keeps coming to his parents' house to beg for food and shelter, then the freedom he claims is immature and unnecessary.

Such has been the faith of African countries. Africans have proved by their behavior that the struggle of their fathers to obtain freedom from their colonial masters was not necessary. Their cry for freedom and liberation from their colonial masters seems ridiculous and pointless. They have proved by their own ways that they did not calculate the burden of their freedom.

It seems that all they wanted was just to get rid of the colonial masters, but they were ill-prepared and were not ready to rule and build their own nations. Though freedom is the joy of the oppressed, it requires a great deal of responsibility for it not to lead to self-afflicted bondage which is the worst kind of bondage.

Nobody wants to be oppressed or afflicted by anyone. It takes a higher energy and power to liberate oneself from a controlling situation, but it takes greater effort, discipline, education, willingness, determination, good planning, greater sacrifice and many more, to maintain freedom in its rightful sense.

True freedom commands respect; it proves that the oppressor was indeed a burden. True freedom promotes value and pride; it gives the platform to release all the hidden skills and abilities and it gives access to the resources a person has, to bring about profitable developments.

Most Black people have abused their freedom. Most Black people do not understand the burden of freedom. Whilst it is good to be free, the freed must realize that the price to pay to maintain freedom is high and it entails hard work and discipline.

"Correct Education of the Black man is Key".
Is the Black Man really free?

CHAPTER FIVE

Race Integrity

Humans have tried to divide themselves through race, but there is just one race, and that is the human race. There is nothing like a White, Black, yellow, red or brown human race. Any classification is just to bring division, control and exploitation among humans. Racism is now controlling humanity and breaking the society. It has taken up residence in the hearts of men, generating hatred and evil among them.

Unfortunately, since it favors some people, the idea is highly supported and fueled by its benefactors. It has killed many innocent people and damaged the lives of very good people. There are over 7 billion people on Earth with beautiful body pigmentation, stature and languages. The languages are so beautiful and distinct that every tribe and nation understands themselves perfectly.

The beauty of the human race is that we can learn one another's language and adapt to one another's environment. Humans are blessed with the ability to think, design and implement. Unlike animals, marriages between humans from different nations produce beautiful 100% humans which continue to enrich the human race.

Over the years, there have been several attempts to divide humans into colors, through teachings to prove that humans are different, one from another. Whilst this is partly true and there is a difference between humans based on pigmentation of the skin, attitudes, beliefs and perception, the concept of difference in the human race has led to different scientific conclusions that some humans are superior to others. Such supremacy concepts are simply calculated plans to promote hatred and war which opens doors for exploitation. Unfortunately, this racial superiority has made its way into the social system and has been embraced and diffused through planned education to establish the racial ideology.

This racial ideology has its grip on people and makes them think that those with certain types of body color, who advanced earlier in industrialization, science, technology and inventions, are different from other people. In years past, the acclaimed 'superior' people engineered the racial superiority and colonized many nations. They enslaved many people and ruled them in their country which was classed or known as **imperialism**. The racial ideology sank into the hearts of men and they started to set classification among men. This act promoted the racial difference among humans, where there was a White race, a Black and brown race and a yellow and red race.

The beauty about today's world is that every nation and tribe and color is doing their best to unite and promote their people, because the only way to break racial attacks is to unite ideas, skills and abilities. Many countries that suffered the racial ideology in the past have become stronger today through united ideas, skills and hard work which have yielded positive fruits for their countries and their people.

Most of the Asian countries have attained higher levels of developments and technology that are amazing. They have earned profound respect among humans and do not suffer racial attacks as they did some years back. Today, China is one of the strongest nations in the world. Though it still has some challenges, it has done things that have earned the country great opportunities in many nations.

Most of the Arab countries like the United Arab Emirates have shocked the world by the immense development they have undergone. Other countries to mention include South Korea, Singapore and Japan. The list is not exhaustive. These nations have brought their people respect around the globe and their countries are considered secured grounds for foreign investment.

The Black man, on the other hand, is still struggling and bathing in tons of excuses. As much as others are uniting to develop, the Black man is dividing to fall. Though there have been many Black men and women who have proven their abilities in science and technology, the Black man is still struggling beyond measure.

Africa has become the begging continent though all evidence shows that it is the richest continent. The people of Africa have refused to do things that would bring regard and respect to their people. There is nothing Africa lacks, whether in human resources or mineral resources, yet the integrity of the people is still compromised. It has taken the Black man too long to arise, too long to prove himself, too long to develop and too long to gain respect. It is by the hard work of some few individuals that the Black man has any credit. Most Black people are still seriously suffering.

Until Black people begin to do as most countries have done to liberate themselves, the Black man will continue to suffer. The Black man needs to liberate himself by winning respect for his people through development in every area. The Black man must stop depending on western support and stop the continuous blaming of the White man for his present state.

Every nation and every people have understood the importance of unity except the Black people. Black people do not value themselves, neither do they value their people. The world cannot wait for the Black man to stand on his feet. He must understand the need to arise and begin to walk. The Black man has sat down for too long and maybe he has become too comfortable with his situation, or perhaps believes that his mission on this Earth is to depend on others. The Black man must seriously examine his ways and think before it is too late. The world has moved on and so must the Black man.

There is much work to be done by the Black man to lift the integrity of his race. There must be general awareness and a deep determination and strongmindedness to desire change. Nobody except the Black man can do this.

"The Black Man must arise and walk depending only on himself for stability"

CHAPTER SIX

The Two Faces of Racism

According to Merriam Webster Dictionary, the word racism means several things including:

- **Poor treatment of, or violence against, people because of their race**
- **The belief that some races of people are better than others**
- **A belief that race is the primary determinant of human traits and capacities and that racial differences produce an inherent superiority of a particular race**
- **A doctrine or political program based on the assumption of racism and designed to execute its principles.**
- **A political or social system founded on assumption**
- **Racial prejudice or discrimination**

The American Educationist **Jane Elliot** said:

There is no such thing as different race; there is only one race, and that is the Human Race.

The war between humans based on racism has prevented us from benefiting totally from one another because some groups believe that they are perfect, superior, and more intelligent than others and know everything, whereas others are excluded from the thinking program because they are referred to as inferior. These thoughts, attitudes and comportments are one of the reasons for endless wars and conflicts between humans.

As stated by Jane Elliot, the human race is just one. If this is the case, where does all the chaos and conflict come from? Some people have used racism to fulfil an agenda which was carefully planned and launched to create confusion in the society.

Racism is a doctrine or political program based on assumption and designed to execute its principles. it is an assumption fuelled by political powers to gain power. It is a doctrine of assumptions. It is used to promote hatred and chaos.

Merriam Webster's definition supports what the American Educationist Jane Elliot said, that there is just one race among men, known as the human race. The different races we see today are therefore based on a political program and assumption.

Adolf Hitler's declaration of his belief in a "**Master Race**" was an indication of the inherent racism of the Nazi movement. By political power, Hitler managed to infuse his ideology of a master race into the people and set them against others who were classed as the inferior race.

Racism is a system used by political powers to turn some people to their favour, by promoting a race as superior over others and favouring them in everything to sustain the ideology. The people, who do not know the obscure agenda of racism, blindly indulge in its principles, fulfilling its scope.

Racism does not necessarily mean White man against the Black man. It can also happen between the White man and another White man, White men versus Black men or Black men against Black men. It is a system, an ideology, which some people who are consumed by political power implement to set confusion among the common people to fortify their seat of government, to obtain votes and gain support to execute their evil plans.

The longest and most successful racial fight has been the one between the White man and the Black man. No one can basically say when it is going to end or whether it will end, because every day, fresh episodes of racial situations emerge which ignite the power of the designed agenda. Both the White man and the Black man are used by this awful system to empower a selected few, who, by the chaos of racism, receive honorary medals and promotions for their successful work. The common White man and Black man, who die on the streets, bringing pains to their families, are never remembered. The question is who will be able to tell humans that there is no such thing as a superior or inferior race, since there is only one common race called humans?

The racial deception has sunk too deep into the hearts of men and has become part of their personalities. It has become an accepted fact, a theory and a concept that is being defended as a heritage. There are men who are going around and promoting this hatred among the people with documented facts and scientific proof to sustain their ideology, knowing very well that they are lies. Most people do not know the hidden agenda behind racism, so, they support it blindly.

Racism is a great weapon which achieves, beyond expectation, what the military cannot achieve. Racism promotes wickedness and sustains political power. It executes all the government laws without struggle and supports every law implemented by the political power. This is one of the reasons why every government who wants to win the approval of a people would do something to promote that group of people knowing that they will succeed without failure as they make some racial statements and moves.

How long shall men swim in ignorance? A lot of time, energy, potential, skills, abilities and knowledge have been wasted on racism. Many people have lost their lives through racism and many more would lose their lives if this evil system is not exposed. Adolf Hitler was able to use the racism weapon to kill millions of people and his people could not see it because he chose a race and promoted them over others.

In the United States of America, racism is still hovering over the nation. The United States, a great nation, powerful, rich, industrious, technologically sound and scientifically advanced, still suffers from racism. Racist venom continues to set the people against each other because the system has become part of the culture. Racism is like a cancerous disease which devours a healthy body until it kills it. It must, therefore, not be allowed in any society because it destroys skills and abilities, potential and talents, the wise and prudent, the strong and the courageous, the beautiful and the perfect.

It puts fear in the mind of people and makes them react based on assumption. Racism grows to become a mind-set which reflects as a character forming a personality. Most people can be classified as racist because they think and behave that way. They act racist because they believe it is right.

According to Jane Elliot,

"No one is born a racist, but people are taught to be racist. White people are taught to behave that way and whatever we learn can be unlearned".

It might sound very harsh, but people learn to become racist regardless of skin color. Those who understand the power of racism use it to fulfill their wicked agenda. We must unlearn racism by reasoning on our own.

On the flip side, there are certain things people classify as racism that are not. There are those who take advantage of the racist atmosphere to lure people into fights to cover up their dirty businesses. That is why it is an obligation for everyone to reason. When reasoning is employed, people cannot be manipulated to be racist.

Sometimes certain behaviors of people are very disturbing, which can cause a person to separate from them. This is not because they are hated, but to avoid problems, and that is not a racist act.

There are people who always invite troubles around them and when you are found in their company, they get you into unwanted situations which can complicate your life; when you avoid such a company of people, it is not a racist act.

There are many people who have isolated themselves from others not because they hate them, but because they decided to avoid suffering brought on by unfavorable acts. If separation could be done on a one-on-one basis, then it could be done as a group, if behavior, acts or conditions are not favorable and that is not racism.

When a Black man who is a lazy worker is fired by his boss who is a White man or vice versa, it must not be interpreted as racism because attitudes, comportment, behaviors and character must always be checked to avoid errors. Certain ways of doing things can make other people avoid your company or involvement with you, not because they hate you, but because they simply cannot stand your ways.

A person cannot be forced, or obligated by the law, to accept bad manners. People have the right to choose whom they should relate with and whom they should not. Likewise, they must behave themselves to be acceptable to others. Unfortunately, some people think they can do what they like and that they must be accepted anyway. When such people encounter a barrier, they call it racism.

When character, comportments, attitudes and behaviors are not checked and corrected, they become a bad smell that marks a person which pushes people away but when a person learns manners and behaves, they attract people. We must not forget that everybody has the right to choose whom they want to relate to. Our own ways would determine whether we are accepted or rejected.

"Racism is an ideology which the Black man must ignore"

CHAPTER SEVEN

The Slave

In Merriam Webster's dictionary, a slave is defined as,

"One that is completely subservient to a dominating influence".

This means that people of influence take those of lesser or no influence and dominate them for their own personal or national agenda. There is no pride in owning another human, yet, the slave trade existed in human civilization for so long.

In this 21st Century, where it seems that knowledge has increased, and human intelligence and understanding has developed, slavery is still practiced in some countries, because it is considered as pride. The purpose of slavery was to show a person's superiority and power, riches and influence. Men travelled from place to place to capture innocent men and women by surprise and, most times, through deception and took them to slave markets to sell them for money. The slave trade was one of the foolish ways in which money was made and it was permissible and highly practiced.

This trade existed for centuries and is still practiced in not so liberal a manner. The slave trade is an old practice that was acceptable among men. Many people have suffered from this awful trade because of its degrading effects.

In its old form, the slave owners enjoyed their human property and treated them whatever way they pleased and never considered the effect it caused in the soul of the slave. Slavery was a trade that brought much gain to the investors. They saw the humans involved as their machines to promote their businesses and they enslaved people either as forced labor in the field or as sources of entertainment in the sex trade. Men and women were abused and sometimes killed because they resisted, were old, sick or unproductive. The owner of the slave only saw money and pleasure at their disposal. Until it was abolished, slavery always promoted racism and segregation. The owners of slaves and their people were considered superior, intelligent, authentic educators and qualified for leadership and governance, whereas the slaves were marked as servants and servants only.

Slavery was the trade, but the slave was the human that was traded. The life of the slave was the most miserable because his purpose in life was channeled to obeying and serving another. He had no right to reason or improve himself except to please his master. What he knew or thought was irrelevant because he was not allowed to contribute any ideas since he was considered as a mechanical force and not a thinking being. The slave was tortured and brutalized when he failed to satisfy or meet his masters' expectations. Any attempt he made to set himself free was considered a foolish act and a serious and unpardonable crime which could be punishable by death. The slave was not allowed to have any future plans because his future was to increase his masters' wealth and happiness.

The wisdom, skills, abilities, potential and knowledge of the slave were sabotaged by his master. The slave was considered a liar whose word against his master in court was considered as verboten. The slave could not have a stable family because his children were owned by his master for more productivity. He had no privacy; neither could he own anything, because his entire existence was to satisfy the desire of his master.

Anything the slave master said about the slave was considered the truth. Many books and articles were written about the slave to educate the masters' people about the inabilities of the slave, his weaknesses, his limited brain and his incapability to govern himself without being directed by his master. What the master failed to acknowledge was that, he had forbidden the slave from doing anything for himself and had passed strict laws to restrict the progress of the slave. The master continuously monitored the slave to make sure he did not have any opportunity to prove his theories about him wrong. The slave now also became a prisoner for life.

In order for the slave master to keep the slave bound forever, even the freed slave continuously bore the name **free slave** in relation to his identity instead of just simply accepting his person. This was because the racial segregation had been created to maintain the ideology of superior and inferior humans. No matter how intelligent the **freed** slave was, his intelligence was not acceptable, neither was there a place for him in the society of his masters.

Unfortunately, humans have failed to understand that there is no such thing as a 'slave'. It is just the wicked nature of man to dominate one another to prove their superiority. No human has the right to enslave another as a personal property.

Every human has the right to be free to develop his potential. The world has now seen that there is no one people having all the skills and abilities in life as we were made to believe, but men from different countries have contributed a lot with their skills to make life better for all.

Though slavery has been legally abolished, the mindset of slavery is still breathing through the world. The physical abolishing of slavery is done, yet the ideology of slavery is still governing the world. The conflict between Black and White is still a problem to be solved. There are still some men promoting racial superiority and segregation and talking about how important it is for people to be separated both socially and academically.

Humans are still confused and are seriously working hard, unwisely, on how to make the world a 'bitter' place to live. Though the leaders of the world keep meeting to promote peace, the outcome of their innumerable meetings show that what we hear in the news is just 1% of their own personal agenda.

It is not only the Africans who have suffered from the wickedness of the slave trade. This horrible trade existed previously in ancient times and many people suffered from its controlling power. The internet is fraught with information on different classifications of slave trade in the ancient past. Nevertheless, it is important for a people to rise above anything that limits them.

Nelson Mandela was kept in prison for almost 27 years with hard labor, which was a type of slavery. When he was released, he had every right to be resentful and accuse his oppressors of injustice and every right to remain embittered. Instead, he renewed his mind and demonstrated a higher level of leadership intelligence. He became the first Black president of a suffering South Africa and he showed all Black people that they had the ability and potential lying dormant within them if they would only overcome the bitterness of their suffering.

Most Black people are still using slavery and colonial rule to hinder their own capabilities. They have become so embittered and have rejected every opportunity given them because they keep blaming the White man.

This mindset that most Black people have has hindered them from developing themselves and their countries. They continue to point fingers and accuse the White man for their condition but what the Black man refuses to understand is that they are in control of their own brain and thus their own destinies. The White man did many wrong and evil things against the Black man; that is true. However, he did not imprison his brain, nor has he stopped him from developing. Though he may pose challenges depending on context and what is needed for development, the Black man has enough determination to win over the challenges posed.

Some years back, most Africans were taken away from their motherland into slavery on foreign lands. The truth is that very few Africans were taken away but amazingly, the whole race of Black Africans behaves as though they were also carried away into slavery. Those who were carried away must know that the suffering of the fathers was to let them have a right in the country they live in and the pride and glory of the fathers is to know that their sacrifices were not in vain. Their fathers did not die to see their children display so much ingratitude by being lazy and unproductive.

Whether in the motherland or the diaspora, the Black man must prove to the world that he has the potential and skills to do great things because the cry for freedom has been heard. The Black man must truly emancipate himself from mental slavery and aim to achieve his main purpose on earth.

No matter how people think about the Black man, all Black people should know that they are not slaves, whether in the motherland or the diaspora. The Black man must not believe all the nonsense that has been written against him and must not adapt to those conditions. Though the Black man looks very different in appearance, the beauty of his color depicts the epitome of an excellent creation. Nobody is born or created a slave. Slavery is man-made and made by greedy men who did not and do not know the essence of life.

"The Black man must rewrite his own story"

Mental Slavery

Mental slavery is a condition whereby a person is incapable of using their own mind to release the abilities to develop. A mentally enslaved person refuses to be productive due to things they painfully experienced or due to thoughts concerning their own personality. The skills of a person can be affected by such thoughts and could portray a bad image about a person.

In his popular redemption song, Bob Marley said to the Black man,

"Emancipate yourself from mental slavery, none but ourselves can free our own mind".

Bob Marley saw that the Black man had a battle against the word slavery and this word had entangled his functionality. The word travelled deep down into his soul to cease his skills and abilities. Bob Marley must have perceived that the word slave became the definition of who the Black man was, and it did not only affect those in America, but it became the identity of the Black man in general. Thus, wherever the man Black man was found, he was seen or represented as a slave. Other people visualizing him as a slave had a negative opinion about him. The opinion of others was not as damaging as the opinion the Black man had of himself. He was now faced with serious identity crises because his image had been stained and his struggle was to free his mind.

Unfortunately, false teachings, awful books, degrading movies and horrible documentary films about how inferior the Black man was, have been diffused, which are not seen by only the Black man, but have become part of the educational syllabus to prove the identity of the Black man.

Slavery has been abolished for quite some time now but the Black man has still not overcome the trauma of slavery. Around the globe, the Black man's functionality has been challenged in many ways; for example, it is either that he is denied the access to show his skills and abilities or he is considered inferior or questionable.

The stigma that surrounds the personality of the Black man has conditioned the Black man not to work hard to break the mental chains of slavery.

Every Black man must break the psychological damage about his identity and strive hard to demonstrate his abilities and skills in excellence. There are some social systems that seem helpful to the society, but basically, it contributes immensely to influence the abilities and skills of people. In some countries, the government gives benefits to people who do not work to help them to survive until they obtain a job. As good as this idea can be, it has allowed a lot of people to fold their arms and totally design their lives around these benefits because they are free. For the benefit reason, many people have refused to put in any effort to improve themselves for a better life. In most of these social benefits' systems, Black people collecting benefit outnumber all other people.

As far as the International Monetary Fund (IMF) and other financial organizations are there to lend money to countries, African countries have built their survival around these systems which has launched them into debts and difficulties. They are not able to manage the great mineral resources given them by nature to develop their countries. Instead, they run for the offers these financial organizations give without considering the consequences.

The Black man has allowed himself to be affected and has permitted a bad image to be created around him. Some people have also gone through similar situations as the Black man that were not favorable, but they worked hard with determination to improve their self-image and won respect among others.

Though the Black man has gone through horrible situations caused by the injustice of others, it is not an excuse for his current state. The Black man must arise and compete through development and display his skills and abilities. The Black man must plan and develop. The image of the Black man is still a struggle due to the many challenges surrounding him, but he must know that he is still responsible for his own failure and success.

As powerful as the mind can be, it can still be blocked by certain patterns of thought. The Bible even says that,

"As a man thinks in his heart (mind), so is he".

What the brain thinks is very important because the whole being responds to it. The things we permit to enter our brain, whether good or bad, go a long way in shaping our attitudes and our performance in life. A person can never be more than how he sees and thinks of himself.

What we believe about ourselves can affect our performance in life, because it continues to control our mind and influence our abilities and skills. From experience and from discussing with parents and colleagues, many children who believed what their teachers said about them concerning their poor performances and their inability to become useful in life, ended up becoming exactly what their teachers said about them because they accepted, believed and thought that way. They became slaves to the words of their teachers. In other words, they were, subconsciously, mental slaves to their teachers. Until the chains of mental slavery are broken, affected people will continue to function below the expected quota of human performances which will cause the society to see them as unfruitful and as a burden.

Higher percentages of Black people are seriously struggling over the slavery issue which has made them forget the strength and potential lying dormant within them. Until there is a clear break from the past with a positive renewed way of thinking, many Black people will remain bound by their own pattern of thought.

Most Black people think that the White man is the cause of their inability to succeed in life, but the fact remains that they have permitted themselves to be controlled by what they have conceived in their minds, which has mutilated them. The trauma of slavery, the pain, the injustice, the wickedness and racism has held the Black man back from freeing his mind and progressing. In as much as he is endowed with potential, the Black man is still struggling to release himself to prove his greatness.

For many years, the Black man has fought to prove his identity and to prove that he is not a slave but equal with any human being on earth. This fight is not necessary because the greatness of a man reveals his identity. The skills, abilities and potential of a man define his identity. Black men who have understood this simple fact have become very successful in life, but the majority are still embittered, struggling to overcome the unfairness and injustice served to their fathers.

It is true that life is not always fair, and many times, life ceases to make sense. It is also true that sometimes, some people who are supposed to know and do better, do worse. Wars and human exploitation make no sense, but they happen. However, every person has the right to rise above the unfairness of life by controlling their mind and demonstrating their capabilities and potential.

Many people have become victims of the unfairness of life and have allowed it to cripple them. Many have become complainers and accusers of others who have managed their way through the unfairness of life. Our brain belongs to us and the managing of it is our responsibility. Since this is the case, no one can accuse another for their own state in life.

"The Black man has not overcome the trauma of Slavery"

The Master Zone and The Slave Zone

A man narrated a situation he encountered that taught him a great lesson. He explained that whenever he traveled by air, he flew in economy class because that was what he could afford. One day, as he boarded the plane, he found that his seat was occupied by another and there was no space for him. The air hostess examined his ticket and realized that the mistake was not his fault. Therefore, the hostess apologized and politely asked him to make his way to business class. That was his first time seeing what business class even looked like.

In business class, he noticed that the people there behaved differently and talked differently, exchanging complimentary cards and talking only about business. The services and attention they received was also different from what he was used to. A man walked to him and asked his name and what he did for a living and he was short of words because he knew that he was there by mistake, not by choice. The next thing he saw was that, after they had spoken for a while, everybody brought out their laptop computer and started to work. One of the men worked the entire journey of 8 hours until the aircraft landed. It was then that he understood why, in this life, some people are rich and some are poor.

The same aircraft had different compartments and there were no restrictions on anyone. It was open to the public by choice, but most people chose to buy the economy class tickets because that was what they wanted, and some chose the first class or business class tickets because that was what they wanted as well. It was all a question of mindset, vision and choices.

In any given country, city or area, there is a slave zone and a master zone available to all. You are the architect of where you live and how you live. The place you choose has the capacity to recondition your perspective on life and it can either reduce or enhance your ability, cage your dreams or expand them, alter your scope of vision and remodel your personality either negatively or positively. The choice is yours to make. The poor always see the rich as the cause of their hardship, but they do not know that they are the cause of their own dilemma.

The way a person thinks reflects his achievements. No one can be more than what he thinks. People who choose to settle in the slave zone and kill their abilities and willpower become bitter about everything and see everything in a negative way. They see others making millions of monies, accumulating wealth and living better, whilst they walk in difficulties and hardships with no solution.

Those who go for business or 1st class in an aircraft pay some more money to have that comfort, which means that, to live in the master zone, a person must put himself under pressure, in other words, go an extra mile in working hard to bring out his best. Whilst some people are sleeping, some are seriously working, some are dancing on the streets and having parties, some are researching and planning for the next ten years to come, others are adapting to a lifestyle of poverty whilst some are creating multi-million-dollar businesses.

One thing that cannot be denied about the White man is that the White man is hard-working. He works very hard and very smart. The White man works hard to maintain his family and his environment as he desires comfort mostly. Just like in any country, there are very notorious ones who are troublemakers, but the hard work of the majority covers the bad ones.

Some Black people are also hard workers who have done incredibly well, beyond imagination, but the majority of Black people have chosen the slave zone consciously or unconsciously to condition their personalities and subject themselves to problems. Most of the Africans that migrated to the Western countries had a slave-zone concept. They came to do all of the domestic and cleaning jobs, looking to the government for social benefits to maintain their families. A few, however, chose the master zone by putting pressure on their lives to educate themselves and enjoy the comfort of the master zone.

No one forbids anybody from having some comfort, but it takes hard work, discipline, determination, vision, planning, sacrifices, education and more to bring out the best in a person to launch them into greatness. Whatever choice a person makes is very important and must be respected, but everyone must be conscious of their choices and must accept responsibility and the consequences of their actions and thoughts, without pointing fingers at others.

> *"The Black man must abandon the Slave zone for the Master zone"*

CHAPTER EIGHT

The White Man and His Conception

I never gave a deep thought to the term **White man** until recently, when I began to carefully observe the operations and the mindset behind it. The term '**White man**' has caused so many troubles in our world and made many people suffer bitterly. When I consider the wasted years and struggles this term has brought among humans, it saddens my heart. The Earth, which should be a place of joy for all people, has become a place of sorrow because humans are still fighting for racial superiority, just like little children from the same family with everyone thinking he is the parent's best child.

The term 'White man' does not necessarily refer to people with White body pigmentation because there are no such humans existing on Planet Earth. The people who call themselves White are not White in pigmentation though Merriam Webster dictionary refers to them as,

> *"A race or people who have light-colored skin that comes originally from Europe".*

In my own definition, a White man refers to a person who considers himself superior in everything as compared to others; someone who considers himself as supreme, pure, infallible, all-knowing and powerful and the best; someone who thinks that he must lead in everything.

This term 'White man' was created by some men to maintain their power and influence over others. This idea was initiated by some rich and influential people who believed that they are the controllers of world affairs and everything must operate according to their pattern of thought.

These rich and influential people set the system in motion and, knowing very well that they would need subordinates, used those with similar body pigmentation as a cover-up to launch their ideas. The system was set in such a way that it was to favor all those with the same kind of body pigmentation as theirs. Most of the people who call themselves White people do not know the agenda behind it. The term is a segregator term used to fuel racial fights, forbidding its kind to help or see those called Black as important. In times past, most White people hated the Black man, not because the Black man did anything wrong, but because they were told to do so. The very poor White people were not considered much because they had little to offer.

The White system protects an ideology which is hidden from the public and it was exclusive to those who were prominent in the society, though the poor White person would benefit. The system succeeded in infusing the idea of racial superiority in society to promote fear which enabled control. Up until today, most White people are still victims of the system. The fear in their heart is still controlling them. The system caused a lot of White people to maltreat the Blacks, especially in the United States and South Africa, and bear false witnesses against them with many Black people killed mercilessly. The White man killed and bullied the Black man for pleasure because the system protected him. Though most of the White people hated what went on, they could not do much to stop what they saw because if they did, the system would come against them and they would suffer like the Black man or anyone the White system disliked.

The system did not fight only Black folks, but anyone who was declared as an enemy. Most White people, who fought battles and hated and killed especially Black people, did so only because of fear of the system. On reflection, many of them expressed their lack of pride in their actions and many deemed some of the wars unnecessary.

White people who knew that the White system was wrong and took a stand to defend the Black man got themselves into trouble. Most White people who hated the system were attacked and their families were marked. They were deprived of the system's protection and were left to suffer. These behaviors of the system's attack caused most White people who hated the system to remain silent.

The system did not only attack different races, as it was made to believe, but attacked countries and any person that it disliked. The system did not allow anyone to control it, but it had the power to control anyone it wanted at any time.

Until today, most White people are still under this spell and they are afraid to relate fully with other people because the system still controls them. They feel threatened and in danger when they see people who are different in their environment because they were told and made to believe that it is only around their people that they would be secure. The White system, therefore, has succeeded immensely in its original purpose to use the people to fulfill its obscured plans. The system makes the White man think that he is better than everyone else and that he is self-sufficient, a superior race and most intelligent, which forms part of the plan.

One of the main agendas of the term 'White man' was to strongly promote racial superiority. By this, anyone who formed part of the White man's group was considered better than any person from any other group of people. In this, many White people have defined themselves clearly, promoting White mans' supremacy over other people. This shows how the White man system or ideology is being protected and nurtured over the years by committed followers. Unfortunately, a lot of the White people are still being manipulated by clever men who are using color differences to define intelligence and smartness.

Since the White man ideology has existed for many years and has taken its root in society, it continues to bear fruit whenever someone rises to plough and water it. There is still a great bridge to cross to bring light on this system because those it favors do not want to lose the benefits they enjoy.

The American Educationist **Jane Elliot** dedicated her life to enlightening people about this error regarding the White race. In an interview, she made it very clear that there was no such thing as different race because there is only one race and that is the human race. She did her best to teach and prove this truth to the entire world. Simply, racism was constructed to promote White supremacy.

Tim Wise, who is an American anti-racism activist, spells out boldly the deception of the White man's ideology and exposes the unfairness between the White man's privileges over the Black man's and the other group of American citizens. As a White man, he saw the need to enlighten the Americans and the world at large about the deception of White supremacy and racial injustice.

Jane Elliot also said,

> *"No one is born racist, but people are taught to be racist. White people are taught to behave that way, and whatever we learn can be unlearned".*

In one of **Oprah Winfrey's** shows, **Jane Elliot** proved to everyone how it felt to be discriminated against. In an experiment she conducted during the show, she separated people who had brown eyes from those of blue and green eyes, and she favored those with brown eyes by giving them attention and benefits, stating also that they were intelligent and smarter than those people with blue and green eyes. The result was unbelievable because White people with brown eyes believed that they were more intelligent than the White people with blue and green eyes and because of that, they merited the best. Most White people realized for the first time what it meant not to be accepted or considered by those who felt superior and better than them.

Having said this, it must be emphasized here that Black people must not allow the injustice that has gone on because of the term 'White man' to cause them to hate all those classified as White people. White people were equally lied to and manipulated to launch an ideology by some clever people to cover their thirst for power and supremacy over others. The people who planned this called themselves White men, and the system favored all those who had the same body pigmentation. After so many years, this conception has remained and become a reality, accepted and practiced everywhere the 'White' man lives. It is defended and promoted, taught and openly declared that the White man is superior to every other group of people on earth, yet the White man bears witness to the fact that knowledge, skills and abilities are not sacred in his camp alone as he was made to believe, but the human race is rich with vast treasures of skills and abilities hidden in people, which are to be shared for the benefit of all.

Apart from the White man's ideology that has painted their image, they are a very wonderful people full of love and kind-hearted. They are good people, caring and determined. They have also contributed positively to better and beautify our world with their skills and abilities. Humanity would not be complete without them because they are talented and great as a people.

Most White people who understood the injustice of the White system stood against the perversion of the system to fight against White supremacy, risking their lives and that of their families. Though the White system is now strong and has become well-developed over the years, a few White men have decided not to rest until the majority of White people come to the knowledge of the deception they have lived for years against other people, most especially, Blacks.

Every group of people has their own troubles and challenges in their own country and, most times, the request of the authorities is what the people execute. White people have followed instructions that have programed their minds to think in a certain way, and just like **Jane Elliot** explained, they have been indoctrinated and not educated on the issue of race and humanity. Therefore, the White man must be understood from his angle of operation because he is good, as are his people. We cannot condemn all White people because of the manipulative ideology that was infused in them. They are simply wonderful people and no matter how hard it might seem, both White and Black and all groups of people, have great work to do towards bridging the racial gap which has separated the human race.

Jane Elliot said, in an interview, that White people are not only educated but they are also indoctrinated. They are made to believe things without any room for analyses. The conceptions they have about Black people were given to them through indoctrination. She said, 'White people are taught to be racist; they were not born racist but were indoctrinated'.

Most White people fear the Black people, not because the Black person has done anything to them, but because of the things they have been taught about them. When a Black man walks in a White neighborhood, everybody expects him to commit a crime. They sometimes immediately call the police to alert them of this intruder whose only purpose in that neighborhood is to do something bad.

They do not expect the Black man to be a lawyer looking for his client, or a private investigator, or a policeman in civilian attire, or a judge going for a walk. They jump to conclusions and describe the Black man as criminal. Fear causes most of them to invent lies to incriminate a Black man just walking on the streets.

The effect of such knowledge is far-reaching. For example, this knowledge made me conscious of my dressing each time I went out of the house as I did not want to be regarded as a criminal. I strongly believe that I am not alone in such thinking and behavior. One day, I packed my car to buy pizza and there was a White family coming towards me with their little children running on the streets. The incentive they applied to catch and restrict the children was to tell the children: 'the Black man is coming, and he will catch all of you and eat you'. The children screamed and ran away from my direction, crying loudly and looking scared, whilst their parents laughed and enjoyed the scene. I looked at them and passed silently without showing any sign of displeasure because I knew the White's conception of Black people.

As another example, some years ago, I bought a used Audi car from a car dealer and on my way to the house, two white policemen on their motor cycles, going in the opposite direction, saw me driving because my windows were down. I had no music on; neither did I drive at speed. They turned, almost causing an accident, and rode towards my car, one in front and the other behind, strictly ordering me to park, which I did immediately. All eyes were on me when they asked me to turn off my engine. They went around the car for some seconds and they asked me for the documents of the car. I provided everything, then they asked me where had I got the car. I said to them, "I just took it from the car dealer 10 minutes ago." They then asked me how much I had bought the car for and I told them. After 30 minutes examining my documents, they came back and said that my car was big and nice, so I could go. I stood there for some time and wondered what on earth the Black man had done to his brother, the White man, to deserve such suspicion and attitude.

As I moved from that place to the supermarket, I saw another group of policemen roaming about the parking lot and as they saw me come out from my car, they blocked me and asked for my car insurance, license and documents of the car. I explained that I had just been examined and investigated by their colleagues 30 minutes ago, but they did not listen. They then asked me where I got the car and how much I had bought it for and I told them. After some minutes of control, they came back and handed over my documents and they left.

I know they were doing their job, but they were expecting to find something wrong with me or my car which they were sure they would get but neither my car nor my comportment fell into their trap. They left disappointed because I did not satisfy their suspicion.

Oprah Winfrey talked about her experience in Switzerland where a bag-shop owner refused to sell a bag to her because she thought it was beyond the reach of Oprah. She insisted that it was too expensive for Oprah to buy and she would not even allow her to touch the bag. That famous and expensive bag that Oprah Winfrey could not buy cost 25,000 Swiss Francs, which was equivalent to 26,000 U.S dollars. Oprah Winfrey, the richest Black woman in the United States of America and a personality of high class, was refused the selling of a bag by a White woman who did not know who she was because of the White conception about Black people. If Oprah had been even a poor White woman, this seller would have allowed her to see and touch the bag the way she liked even when the bag was not eventually bought.

The conception the White man has of the Black man is very bad, and this has affected the minds of other people against the Black man. Many people look down on the Black man because the White man has written so many things to complicate his life.

An Asian man was asked what his view was about the Black man and he explained that he was afraid of the Black man because he is strong. That is why the Black man is good at athletics and can also sing, but he did not think that the Black man was good at anything else. The interviewer asked him why he said those things and his response was, 'I watched them in movies and documentaries'.

It is paramount that the Black man must overcome his limitations and arise to reveal his potential in all fields of life. He must check his attitudes and character not to fall into the many bad conceptions around him. It is to be noted that though the Black man must make positive changes, the White man must also make some serious changes to his attitudes and behaviors towards the Black man for slavery to be truly abolished.

Jane Elliot rightly explained that White people are indoctrinated. She said that we can unlearn what we have learnt wrongly. This applies to both the Black man and the White man. The White man must begin to renew his mind on issues concerning the Black man. What the White man must understand is that, if the situation turns to his disfavor, he would dislike being treated as the Black man is currently being treated.

The Golden Rule in Life is, do unto others what you want others to do unto you.

It is my strong belief that the White person would not like to experience the injustice that the Black man has been served over the years due to misinformation passed on from generations. Whenever a person hears good things about something or someone, there is an instinct that drives the person to relate and know more about that thing or person but when the information about that thing or person is wrong, naturally it sets off an alarm to raise a protective and suspicious barrier. Many people have raised suspicious and protective walls against the Black man but never gave him the chance to prove himself. Reconciliation is a two-way affair that must be entered by both the Black man and the White man.

"The White man must renew his mind on issues concerning the Black man"

CHAPTER NINE

The 'Black' Man and His Conception

Most of the books written by Black people throw the blame of the Black man's problem onto the White man and though the White man made life unpleasant for the Black man living with him, most Black people have folded their arms and have bitterly blamed the White man for their condition. It is very sad to read about some of the injustices that some Black people suffered and are still suffering under the White man's leadership, yet we must not forget about the superb achievements some Black people have attained by overlooking the racial lines.

As long as Black people continue to see White people as the source of their problem, all their energy will be centered on proving to the White man that they are equal. This has been the error over the centuries because there is nothing that the White man is, that the Black man is not. Instead of using their abilities, skills and potential to affect their environment, the Black man's anger and pain have not allowed him to excel because they keep limiting him in many ways. As explained earlier, many Black people have succeeded in this life by understanding that the White man does not own their brain and skills. However, the majority of Black people are still living under the status quo because they are not able to let go of the injustice that persecuted their soul. The cry for vengeance and fight for equality keeps restraining the Black man from digging deeper into themselves to release their potential for better lifestyle.

Whilst the African abroad is fighting for equality, the African in the Motherland is also blaming the White man for his undeveloped state due to colonization. The Black man in the Motherland holds the White man responsible for lack of food, bad roads, poor infrastructures and poverty. The White man, therefore, is the African man's nightmare.

This ideology has restricted the Black man's abilities and potential because he refuses to see himself as responsible for his own condition. As much as the slave trade is hated and should never have happened, it was not all Africans who were carried away into slavery. However, all Africans behave as if they were all in slavery, and therefore, the White man must compensate them and give them all support and attention because he was responsible for their suffering.

Potential and skills, abilities and knowledge lie within people and it takes deep thinking, self-discipline, determination, sacrifice, education, will-power, hard work and many other attributes to unlock them. In the Holy Bible, King Solomon wrote in his Proverbs,

"A Man's gift makes room for him and brings him before great men".

This wise proverb contains the truth about every individual's success. Knowledge, gifts, talents, skills, abilities, and potential are embedded in a person, and these, when discovered and developed, bring them into greatness. Complaints and accusations, excuses and blame do not make anyone great and they do not put food on the table; neither do they make a man successful. Unfortunately, this is what the Black man is bent on doing.

No matter what the White man has done in the past or present, it is still not a valid excuse for the Black man to suffer or remain poor. The African Legend, Nelson Mandela, said,

"Poverty is not an accident. Like slavery and apartheid, it is man-made and can be removed by the actions of human beings".

Any man-made situation can be removed by man's actions. Therefore, a permanent man-made condition in a man's life is a desired condition. Every man has the right to decide how he wants his life to be by the actions he undertakes. Nobody must blame another for his permanent condition because there is always room for change. Most Black people have conceived a conception about the 'White Man' that has become a limitation in their minds, and, as they refuse to do anything about it, their lives have been halted by this conception.

As a young African man growing up, the conception that ruled my thoughts, which was and still is the belief of a higher percentage of African-born Black men, was that the only way I could be successful in life was to travel abroad to any western country. My environment never taught me to see any good thing in me from which I could develop my life except to travel to Europe or America. My mind was conditioned to function that way because I allowed it to be programed that way and because it was programmed that way, I could not see any other way to succeed in life. I joined the squad of Black man limitations and attributed my condition as being the White man's fault. Then, I asked myself these very important questions;

Who brought me to Europe? Did I come by myself or was I forced by the White man? Is the White man holding my brain from thinking or did I have the right to think on my own? Has the White man held my potential or am I busy fighting for my rights?

As I pondered on these questions, I began to study on my own, observing and conducting researches. I discovered that there are a lot of potential hidden in every man, but it will take deep thinking, self-discipline, hard work, determination, education, sacrifices, responsibility and perseverance to unlock these treasures residing in the man. There is a lot of hard work needed to succeed and greater works more to maintain the success achieved. Nothing good comes easy.

There are some weak conceptions the Black man must break from his mind to release his potential, skills and abilities to enable him to affect his environment. Treasures are in two forms: good treasure or bad treasure. Each of these, when kept, remains the accumulated wealth of the possessor. Most Black people have accumulated bad treasures which consist of pains, sorrows, excuses, accusations, bitterness, anger, injustice, and many more. These are valued wealth in their souls, which has covered the beauty of their personalities causing them to do things which do not reflect their image in the positive sense.

Speaking to many Black people over the years, I discovered the struggle they still have, which is that they see the White man as the reason for their condition. The Black man needs to take responsibility for his actions. For change to happen, he must start to see himself as equal and able to change any man-made conditions in his life. Until he ceases to blame the White man for his poor state, there will be no room for development.

"The Black man must stop blaming the White man"

CHAPTER TEN

Lampedusa

Lampedusa is an island in southern Italy that lies in the Mediterranean Sea, a beautiful place known for its beaches, an egg-laying site for marine turtles and a playground for dolphins. The shallow waters and colorful marine life make this a place of attraction where tourists can enjoy a colorful vacation. In Lampedusa, the water is blue and clear.

Italy is one of the European countries that the Mediterranean Sea divides from the northern part of the African continent, and therefore, most of the North Africans can reach its shore by ship or even boat. In recent times, the island has become known as the **Island of the Immigrants** because thousands of people from North Africa have flooded the island to enter Europe. Reports say that over 20,000 people have lost their lives on the sea by just trying to cross the waters.

Over 85% of these immigrants are Black Africans risking their lives to enter Europe where they believe their lives would be better than remaining in their Motherland. The arrival of these Africans, with pregnant women and children, on the shores of Lampedusa is overwhelming. The Italian coastal guards have rescued thousands of African immigrants who have left their countries to enter Europe, not through the right procedure by acquiring a visa permit but through the waters risking their lives and that of their children to run to the people they call White men for rescue; those who do not like them, who colonized their countries and from whom they liberated themselves and attained independence, who apparently have caused all their troubles. They run to the White man to rescue them from their own people who rule their land.

When they enter Europe, Black people are treated as refugees, separated from society and limited in movement and operations.

Yet, they believe that their lives will be better than remaining in the Motherland. In Italy, most of these Africans go around begging for money on the streets to allow them to eat. Young boys in their prime cannot see any way to live rather than to beg for money and food for survival. Most of the girls are forced into prostitution to make quick money and some of the men into drug-peddling.

From what can be seen, the White man is not responsible for these behaviors. In talking to some of these Black people, their aim in life is to make money through whatever means, no matter the cost. Released videos on Facebook, WhatsApp and personal testimonies shared by these immigrants show the immense price they pay to cross the seas. Some of the stories are better untold.

Regardless, thousands more Black Africans flood Libya and the surrounding North African shores to cross to Europe. According to eye witnesses, these Black Africans are maltreated like slaves, beaten and sold to other merchants for money if they cannot afford the fares required to cross the sea, and those who have money pay for their trip on these dangerous waters to Europe.

The question is, what is wrong with the Black man? No matter what anyone says, there is no White man with guns in the African countries chasing the Africans to Europe for slavery, but this time, the Africans themselves run from their own countries, begging the Europeans to save them.

There is nothing wrong when people migrate from one place to another, because it contributes to enriching a nation with diverse skills but when a mob of people run from their own countries to enter another country without the proper procedure, it is no longer regarded as migration but invasion. Black Africans invade Europe and many Asian countries in their masses to escape from the leadership of their own brethren and most of them worsen their conditions due to the unexpected life that they live abroad.

Though there are some Africans who are very influential in the western world, the majority of Blacks are still bent on domestic and cleaning jobs as if that is the only field of work in which they can be successful. This reveals the image that the Black man has of himself. The power to think and create is not given to the White man alone but it is demonstrated by any person who has understood their purpose in life and has activated their skills and talents through deep thinking.

Great thinkers are the ones who have affected our world. Whatever a man needs to succeed in this life is wrapped inside him, but it takes deep thinking to discover these hidden treasures and it takes hard work, determination, sacrifice, discipline, education, focus and many more to unleash this potential. Every successful person in our society, whether Black or White, applied these principles to succeed because it is certain that in this life, nothing **just** happens.

It is believed that the African has not fully understood life and its purpose. As discussed in the chapters above, the Black man's conception about life has limited him in many things. The Black African is blessed with great knowledge and potential just like any other human being, but most Black Africans believe that their survival would only come from the western world. For this reason, they shut the doors to discovering their hidden treasures and they throw themselves at the mercy of the White man to make ends meet.

The crossing of the Mediterranean Sea from North Africa to Lampedusa has become a great business. The White man did not go to bring Black people from their homes with guns, but Black people travelled willingly, paying any price just to enter Europe knowing very well the consequences awaiting them.

Thus, it can be concluded that the slave trade is reopened in North Africa and Black people are the main products. In the name of Europe, Black people are ready to go through anything to enter, although their stay in Europe is not very secure since most of them have no qualifications or education to allow them to integrate into the European working society and even if they have, they still cannot operate because of improper documentation. Black peoples' lives in Europe are a nightmare; yet, thousands are still selling themselves to enter Europe.

If the White man is that bad towards Black people, why are Black people running from their own countries to join the White man in his own country? Why would a mother take her child to cross the sea in an unsafe boat to Europe? What is happening in Africa? Why is it that the African youth's dream is to come to Europe?

The easiest way to avoid responsibility is to accuse others. The pointing of fingers to blame others causes a person not to realize their own fault. The Black man has accused the White man for so long that he has refused to see the gap being created between them. The more the White man is accused, the more he excels and the more the Black man accuses the White man, the more he runs to the White man for his help. For how long will this game continue? What is wrong with the 'Black Man'? There are still many things the Black man has to accomplish which do not require the help of the White man, but the Black man has refused to take and accept responsibility for applying the basic principles of life.

"The Black man must accept responsibilities for
his own actions"

CHAPTER ELEVEN

Who Rules Africa?

The colonial rule over Africa ceased some years ago because great men who saw the potential residing in Africans fought their ways to liberate Africa from the colonial system. They believed in their people and they knew that, with hard work, they could bring their countries out of poverty into abundance. They knew that the Black man could govern his own people. The White man reluctantly withdrew from African soil and concentrated on strategies to develop their own countries.

Africa is known for beauty, due to the unique body pigmentation which her people have that is different from all other people, and for the immense amount of treasure embedded in her soil. Without controversy, Africa is the richest continent on the planet.

The colonial masters left the governance of Africa to the Africans which was the right thing to do. Since then, Africa has been fully governed by Black Africans, except South Africa, whose case was different because the White man did not only colonize them but became citizens and ruled the country in favor of the White man; but even that has now also changed. Black men have had full control over the continent for some years now, negotiating affairs that benefit the nation.

Black men ruling their own countries were expected to bring quicker developments and stability by making good decisions and profitable negotiations that could ease their economy just as their great fathers dreamt and trusted by their sacrifices. However, though the Black man now has full power over his own countries, his economy continues to sink, and poverty continues to rise above controllable levels. In many African countries, there is lack of food and drinking water, many sicknesses and diseases and the rate of illiteracy is high. Though the

Black man has abandoned his farming and craft jobs and other jobs related to his talents to pursue 'white-collar' jobs, there are no 'white-collar' jobs for graduates and no support for creative abilities.

The thirst for power invaded Africa, and military men continuously fight for the seat of government. This, unfortunately, has increased the economic instability of African nations which scares foreign investors. Previously, the government negotiations with the western world were made to improve the African economy. However, Africa continues to sink and soak herself in debt, thus impoverishing her people.

In defending themselves, the African leaders shift the blame for their inability to lift the nations out of their darkness onto the White man. The White man, once again, is responsible for not allowing the Black man to survive in his own country ruled by his own people. This indicates that though the Black man is physically seen as governing his own country, in reality, the White man rules the country. This is one conception that many Africans agree on, though I beg to differ, and I strongly believe I am not alone in such disagreement.

The Black man is responsible for his own actions. The leaders of African nations are the ones ruling Africa. The White man does not rule Africa. Negotiations are made to bring profit, advancement and peace to individuals or nations. African leaders make their own decisions and negotiations. They had, and still have, the right to reject any decision or negotiations that would not benefit the nations. If they engaged themselves in anything about their nations, then it means that they examined the benefit of the negotiations or decisions made. Africans and their leaders have minds of their own, functioning like everyone else. Therefore, it would be incorrect to suggest that the White man rules Africa. The thinking that the White man still rules Africa is one conception that has degraded the abilities of African leaders.

White men do not rule Africa, because Africa is ruled by Black African men who have their own functioning brains, just like every other leader in the world. The difference between the Western Leaders and the African Leaders is their pattern of thought and vision. Without controversy, the economic situation of every country is because of the vision and pattern of thought the government and the people have and Africa is not exempt.

Africa's situation must not be treated as if Africa does not measure up to standard when it comes to the human ability to think. It should not be treated as though Africa needs supplementary thinkers to aid her to rise to the level of human creative achievements. Unless African leaders and their people declare openly that they are incapable of thinking and incapable of implementing their own ideas, under no circumstances can the White man assume the responsibility for, or be blamed for, Africa being underdeveloped.

The Western governments have the right to make negotiations and decisions that will benefit their countries just like every good government would. Therefore, if they make a deal with the African leaders that brings profit and benefits to their own countries, then they should be given credit and allowed to enjoy their hard work. The White man, therefore, owes no one any apology because the African leaders also have the right to make profit over the negotiations which they make. It must, however, be acknowledged that stringent measures may perhaps limit African leaders from making profitable deals. If that be the case, then yes, some responsibility can be cast on the White man for limiting Africa's progress, but the African leaders still need to be deep-thinkers as any situation can be changed by effecting appropriate leadership principles, including deep thinking.

Whenever the Western countries are blamed for the exploitation of Africa under the Black man's leadership, it gives a negative image about the African leaders. It suggests that the African leaders are not deep-thinkers.

It shows that the African leaders do not care about their own nations. It suggests that the African leaders are not intelligent enough to undertake negotiations that would benefit their countries. It indicates that African leaders are selfish leaders. It suggests that African leaders are not competent enough as leaders to lead others. It also suggests that African leaders do not know their duties as leaders. Of these, the worse one is that it suggests African leaders are not smart leaders.

That is why it is humiliating to attribute the African underdevelopment to the White man because it degrades the African leaders. Though some Black leaders, in general, might have some difficulties dealing with certain issues, they must boldly accept responsibility and never throw blame on others. Instead, they must seek for solutions that are profitable.

In the lyrics of his song entitled **Could You Be Love**, the Reggae king, Bob Marley made a bold statement, saying,

"We've got a mind of our own so go to hell if what you're thinking is not right".

He simply implied, according to my own interpretation, that everyone has a mind of his own to think; therefore, another man's opinion must not be the final and the right decision to follow. Africans have the obligation to use their brain to think and not just to accept and follow everything being said by others, because our failure to think gives power to others to decide how we should live, what we can do and when and where we are permitted to operate or function.

All Africans and Black people all over the world must know that we rule our own lives and not the White man. We are responsible for the way we live and the things we do and most of all, the way we think.

"The White man does not rule Africa but the Black man"

CHAPTER TWELVE

Patriotism (The Love for My Father's Land)

When people love their country, as many do, they go the extra mile to defend and develop it. They respect their homeland and acknowledge it as their place of origin, the land of their Fathers, their inheritance and therefore, they stand for it and fight for it.

The love that people have for their country can be referred to as PATRIOTISM **(Merriam Webster Dictionary).**

The preservation of national resources and the developments that are in most countries indicate how patriotic they are. Good leaders build their countries with well-defined structures that are beneficial to the people. Everyone in the country contributes to maintain proper orders which are respected by all.

The love for one's country is very necessary because it engineers sacrifices and vital contributions that stimulate developments. People who love their country build and protect it with meticulous detail. There are countries that are well-constructed and highly protected by the people to maintain their beauty and uniqueness.

Patriotism makes a people invest their time, knowledge, strength and resources into developing their country. There are nations that were broken down because of wars but the people arose and built their nation to be better than before.

Singapore is one of the most disciplined nations in the entire world. They are very patriotic. The people defend their country with teeth and claws and they warn everyone who visits the country to observe the rules and laws of the country before entering because there are no exceptions for law-breakers.

Many other countries show similar patriotism. Though every country has its own challenges, the people work hard to help maintain the name, beauty and social standard of the country.

The South Koreans helped their country out of economic crisis back in 1997. People from all walks of life contributed, from housewives queuing for hours to donate their wedding rings, to athletes donating their medals and trophies, to many others who gave their gold to help their country out of difficulties. This was great patriotism. The people loved their country so much that they were ready to do anything to help her stand strongly again.

Western countries and some of the Asian countries are called advanced countries because of patriotism. The people sacrificed to help their countries. They also laid down structures that helped them to maintain beautiful nations to live in and with good social status. Europe is well-constructed and strong because the people understood that it is not only the duty of the government to maintain a healthy economy and a beautiful country, but that the people also have a collective responsibility to preserve the Father's Land.

There are, however, many countries whose people are not patriotic because they have not understood the value of their Father's Land and they are ready to sell it for shillings. There are people who have betrayed the trust of their country by revealing vital information that is the nation's secrets for very little recompense. Leaders of some countries have only added to the pains and sufferings of their people and the country. They either do not care, or do not even consider the consequences of their actions. Instead, they think only about themselves and what they can get but never what they can do for their country.

Considering how the nations have been exploited by the Africans themselves, one may ask whether Africans understand the word 'patriotism'. Africa, the richest continent on Planet Earth, though most of her people remain poor and underdeveloped, throws red light and raises suspicious alarm. One may ask, do the African people hate their country so much? Or does it not mean anything to them? It is just like a rich man who has a very big and enviable house full of great things, but the house is dirty, broken, not cared for and practically uninhabitable.

The Europeans always make where they live like their homeland by setting up structures and cleaning and protecting the zone allocated to them because of their patriotic mindset. It is easy to see people who are not patriotic when you enter their environment. One could easily notice how shattered the environment appears to be and how the people live and behave.

Patriotism, therefore, is a mindset; it is the extent of love that people have for their country and for their people, to preserve their Father's land, their inheritance, their habitation, their origin and their homeland. Patriotism must be taught to positively give a person the right education on how to contribute to the development and maintenance of their Father's Land.

Most Africans do not even know the value of their country let alone contributing to its development. Some of the leaders of the nations of Africa misunderstood their leadership role for an opportunity to rid or suck their country dry of its resources to enable them to build their lives abroad. The various stories around African leadership leave a big question mark in one's mind; "are African leaders patriotic"?

Do the African people understand or demonstrate patriotism? As a young African growing up in my country, there was nothing I learnt, or I was told that made me love my country or that made me want to contribute to its development. I wanted to go to Europe or America since I heard of how great the place was and the wonderful stories that surrounded them. I never saw anything good in my Father's Land and nothing challenged me because the people I was surrounded by did not live or do differently.

I saw environments that were so dirty and broken, yet people lived comfortably, drinking and eating, because that was normal. There were areas that were not accessible to vehicles though people lived there, and this was normal too. Poverty, sickness, death, illiteracy, corruption, bribery, and stealing were all normal. Injustice, lack of human rights and spiritism were all normal life to me. Everybody did what they liked, where they liked and when they liked, and all these were normal.

I used to ask myself who we were waiting for to help us clean our environments and properly plan our infrastructures before things got out of hand. People built where they liked and how they wanted without any proper town planning. The roads were so bad, supply of electricity was poor, just as was water supply, food and sanitation systems were poor and there was a high level of illiteracy. Many of these still exist today. Nothing has really changed for the better except in child mortality which seemed to have reduced in many countries. Do Africans really love their country? Africa is so blessed as a continent with all that a people would need or ever desire but the people do not see the value of what they have and so cannot maintain what they cannot see or acknowledge.

Dubai has proved their patriotism to the entire world. The developments they have brought into their country call for global recognition and applause. Their patriotism is so incredible because the people have decided to develop their homeland and make it comfortable for all to live in.

There are other countries and people who have chosen to destroy their countries with war in this 21st Century. They have chosen to break down everything they have and make life very difficult for themselves. After they destroy their countries, they move in convoy to other countries, who know the value of patriotism, for help. It is important that every group of people know the value of their Father's Land to develop it for the benefit of all. Until a people become patriotic, they tear down and mess up what they have and always look to others for help. One of the differences between stable developed countries and unstable underdeveloped countries is patriotism. There are those who are very proud to belong to their country and those who do not want to have anything to do with their country. When some people move out of their country, they feel ashamed to even identify themselves with their country of origin because of how things are done there.

Patriotism is a mindset that is not only shown towards the country of origin alone but extends to every place a person or people dwell. Patriotic people see to the development of the place they live or chose to live, because the progress of a nation is progress of all. Africans must first see the blessing they have to relate to their continent. The love they have for their continent should be revealed by the care they have for their nations and how they defend and represent it globally. The development of a nation does not rest only on the shoulders of the leaders but also on those of its people. It is the responsibility of all the people to contribute to elevate the nation's pride.

As of Tuesday 12th September 2017, the population of Nigeria rose to 192,828,961 million as compared to some of the countries below at the same time:

South Korea – 50,744,701

Japan – 125,989,142

United Kingdom – 65,589,625

Germany – 80,626,863

Switzerland – 8,468,609

France – 64,992,158

Italy – 59,797,373

Spain – 46,071,254

Belgium – 11,457,940

Netherlands – 17,043,369

Sweden – 9,934,092

Norway – 5,342,178

Poland – 38,557,642

United States of America – 326,934,867

Australia – 24,705,434

United Arab Emirates (Dubai) – 2,847,925

Russia – 143,984,196

Canada – 36,697.009

Austria – 8,596,917

These results show how populated Nigeria is, which makes it a great opportunity for marketing and for the development of the country. Nigeria's population is more than any of the European countries and the resources Nigeria has cannot be compared to any of the European countries. Yet, the country is in serious difficulties with all the privileges it has and with its population and natural resources which are meant to be positive attributes. This situation is similar to almost all African countries. As big as the United States is, their population is 326,934,867, which, compared to Nigeria, is a little less than double its population.

The population of Nigeria is a big advantage for the country, as is the case with most African countries. However, bad leadership and lack of patriotism has scattered African people around the globe, which is simply opportunities thrown away. The entire population of Switzerland is not even 10 million people, but their country is one of the best countries in the world. Similarly, Norway's population is less than 6 million people and they enjoy a wonderful and beautiful country. Its inhabitants live mostly in snow but the love for their country has made them maintain the pride of the nation.

There have been numerous wars among the Europeans and many difficulties during the building of their countries, but the love they had for their countries was more than the obstacles they encountered. They planned their countries and developed every part of them to make things easier for everybody. The population of Australia is less than 25 million people and still Australia is a great nation and well-developed as a continent.

Black people must face the fact that the love they have for their nations is so small that they do not really care what happens in the country as long as they get what they want. It is sad to say but the realization that Africa's resources are being syphoned and sold to countries abroad is sickening, especially when Africans then go abroad to try to reap from these same resources syphoned from the same Africa that they left behind.

While the countries fall apart, the leaders of African nations are so rich that they have to save their monies in the western banks because the national banks are too small to contain them. Among the many problems in Africa, lack of patriotism is a great factor that needs to be acknowledged and addressed.

There is a need for real patriotic leaders who would become good examples to the people on how important it is for a people to love their country and help it in every way possible. There must be an educational system that will teach the people to love their country, to protect and to develop it. The progress of the country must not be thrown on the government alone but on all the people who must be involved in building their Father's land. The African nations must be loved by both the leaders and the people. The development of the nations must be done with pride by both governments and the people who dwell in the nations. Good practice from Europe and other developed countries must be emulated rather than envied and begged for. Whatever is seen in Europe or in any developed country could be reproduced in any African country if the love for the country is made a priority.

There are some Africans who are very rich and could help to bring change in their individual countries, but they fear the mindset of the majority, so they choose to keep quiet and take advantage of the mess. Some leave the country because they see it as the best way to avoid political attacks, even though they love their country. Such action has made Africa a land for the survival of the fittest. For many reasons, including that of safety, many Africans have abandoned their homeland and sought peace and safety abroad when these same individuals would have been able to help develop the continent. Africa's problems are multiple, but with patriotism, we can start to help Africa develop. Black people are aware of their situation worldwide, but the mindset of finding someone who is responsible for their condition has forced almost all to remain idle. Many believe Africa is a lost cause. Those on the continent who have every power to change things are engaged in things that have nothing to do with development. There is nothing that Africans need that is outside Africa because everything a person would desire is given to Africa without measure. Africa is blessed. It will take the love for a country to repair Africa and its people must be ready and willing to sacrifice for the nation.

Patriotism is one of the great differences between Blacks and Whites. Africans [Blacks] have the power to develop themselves in everything and break the bonds or lift themselves out of poverty and build their nations if they want to. The reggae king Bob Marley said in one of his songs,

'Where there is a will, there is always a way'.

Africans need to be willing and ready to love one another. This is the first step to helping Africa develop. Africans must pool their resources together and have one mind to build. If the UAE can do it, then any African country can do it. Africans must stop being dependent on others as if they have nothing and they must look into and around themselves to discover and acknowledge the numerous, untapped and uncultivated riches that they have, and must develop themselves. It starts with patriotism.

"The Black man must adopt a patriotic mindset"

CHAPTER THIRTEEN

A Coin Has Two Faces

In one of Dr. Martin Luther King Jnr's dreams he had for America, he said,

> *"I have a dream that one day my four little children will live in a nation where they will not be judged by the color of their skin but by the content of their character".*

He made it very clear that it was foolishness to judge a person by the pigmentation of their body instead of the content of their character. The human soul is a treasure full of potential and it has no color. Therefore, it is eternally wrong to cast judgment based on a person's appearance instead of the richness of his character.

In every society, there are good people and bad people of the same body pigmentation and that does not have to thwart judgment because when favoritism and racism pervert the course of justice, the society becomes unstable. Martin Luther King Jnr boldly said,

> *"Let every man be judged by the contents of his character".*

This is because our character reveals our identity.

In as much as there has been cruel injustice against Black people, there have also been very bad character exposures by the same.

Persecution is where a person does the right thing and is attacked by others, whiles prosecution is where a person is attacked by others for the wrong thing they have done. Sometimes, people exchange prosecution for persecution using their color as an excuse.

Most Black people, knowing very well the racial difficulties for Blacks, capitalize on that to do their evil deeds and when later they are prosecuted, they turn it to be racial attack. It is vital that a man develops his character in positive ways in a corrupt society to avoid wrong judgment. Sometimes, due to the White man's conception in the minds of the Black people, Black people behave in such ways that make them commit crimes which could easily be avoided.

Most of the behaviors and attitudes the Black man displays cause limitations on him. The Black man must overcome racial difficulties and develop his attitude and character to enable him to look unique in a world that sees him with suspicious eyes.

The White man and other ethnic groups also have seriously bad attitudes and poor behaviors. However, since the conception of the Black man is more diffused and negative, the Black man becomes more monitored. Unfortunately, the Black man also, by some of the things he does, makes his accusations more credible.

Anywhere around the globe, there are certain things that are commonly noticed about the Black man. Most times, his environment is broken down because he expects someone to fix it for him. It is others' responsibility but not his. If others do not fix it, then it becomes a racial issue. Most Black residences are deprived of proper facilities and often, the Black man expects someone with authority to sort this out. If it is not sorted, then it becomes discrimination.

Mostly, the Black man looks to the government to provide everything he needs, which makes him easy prey. When the government provides everything you need for you, then that gives them the power to control your everyday movements and allow them to decide how you should live.

Just as was discussed in previous chapters, most Africans think that their survival and progress in life is in the hands of the White man and therefore, they refuse to think and strive to release their potential. Instead, they channel their concentration and energy in hoping for help by begging.

The Black man must take up serious responsibility for his own success in life and stop depending on others. There are many White men who believe that the White man is more intelligent than the Black man and they speak boldly of this. If the Black man continues to shut his potential out and continually cry for help, then their conception becomes a theory. The only way the Black man can disprove this conception is by becoming aware of the seriousness of his condition.

Most of the adverts on television to help children are connected to Africa. It seems as if there are no Presidents and leaders in Africa that are aware of the situation in their country. It is amazing to know that there are millionaires and billionaires in Africa among Black people.

The White man launches campaigns for mobilizing funds to give clean water to Africans. The question is, what are the Africans doing? What is wrong with us? We boast of intellectuals and thinkers and riches and minerals and all the wealth in the world but if we cannot give clean water to our people and we allow thirst and hunger to afflict the people then where are we heading?

People sleep in darkness because there is no electricity during the night. Very poor sanitation and low standards of living afflict Black people in their own countries. These things must not be addressed by the Westerners for Africa because they are not going to be used by them. The Africans must see the need to take responsibility to develop their own nations without being a burden to others.

It is irresponsible for the Black man to cast his difficulties and struggles onto the White man because the Black man also has a mind of his own. The Black man is responsible for his own attitude, character and behavior, development and success and, of course, his own failures. The easiest way to remain idle is to shift responsibilities onto others by accusing them wrongly.

Thomas Sankara of Burkina Faso told his people that they could do it if only they were willing to sacrifice and pay the price. He is one of the young African leaders who shook Africans into realizing the potential within them. The change he brought to his people was too much of a price to bear for the development of the nation because it involved hard work and deep thinking. He was killed by his own people and all the effort he made to build the country on self-commitment was rejected by his successor. His successor restored the country back to their colonial masters and declared his inability to lead the country without them. He literarily begged for acceptance. His successor had a mind of his own and he did what he believed the nation needed and that was to beg for food and livelihood. Since he performed his own negotiations as an African President, he cannot shift the blame of his country's condition onto anyone. Why do people strive to become leaders of others if they do not know the value and mechanism of leadership? The Black man must surround himself with a cloud of integrity that reflects his abilities and potential.

It is impressive to see some of the great work many Black people have achieved around the globe. Examples are cited in later sections of this book. These should be examples to all Black people to work hard. Still, the majority of Black people are swimming in difficulties. The behaviors and attitudes, characters and comportments of most Black people are difficult to understand.

One day, I was on the train from Bergamo to Brescia in Italy, and in my coach, there were other Black brothers and some White Italians as well. The ticket controller came in and started asking for tickets and when he asked one Black man for his ticket, the man was agitated and started shouting that the ticket controller was racist because he asked him for his ticket. The controller explained to him that it was not about racism but a routine ticket check. He explained that he had asked the others and none of them had accused him of racism. The Black man insisted that the ticket controller was racist because he asked him first to show his ticket before asking the White guys. The noise was so much that I was very ashamed of the embarrassing situation. When the police eventually came, it was discovered that he had no ticket and was asked to get down from the train. His behavior left an embarrassing perfume on the other Black people on the train.

Certain things Black people do cause others to look down on us and, though it is sometimes very difficult to admit, there is a clear line between racial attack and justice. Most Black people, knowing very well the tension over racial issues, do things to take advantage of the tension, ignoring the consequences. There have been instances when Black people have fallen for such misconceptions and have been involved in unnecessary fights for justice. Black people must condemn anything done by a Black fellow that is wrong by making them know the consequences it has on all Black people. We should not always turn the coin only one way because every coin has two faces. Some of the attitudes and behaviors of most Black people are questionable.

"The Black man can be devious"

CHAPTER FOURTEEN

Rise and Fall

Many stories and researches have highlighted the influence of the Black Man on the planet in times past. Black personalities did great things and challenged the course of human life though their stories are untold. This makes it feel as though we live in a world contributed to only by the White man with no contributions from anyone else.

The White people must be admired not because of how they present themselves by claiming to be wiser than everyone but because of how smartly they have operated. The smartness and intelligence they have displayed so far must be applauded. Careful consideration reveals that the White man is not necessarily wiser than the Black man, or any other group of people, but simply operates smarter. Almost everything about human life is represented by a White man even if it has had nothing to do with him.

I watched Tarzan, a White man who lived in a jungle, jumping from tree to tree, controlling and talking to animals, whilst the indigenous people were afraid of the jungle. How a White man managed to live in the jungle amazed me.

The White man went to Africa and saw the Africans worshipping a huge gorilla, and the gorilla killed all the Black beauties in Africa that were offered it and fell in love with a White blonde lady. Some few White men were able to capture this huge gorilla which the thousands of Africans could not catch or kill, and they took it to America for their entertainment. The question is, what happened to the Africans?

The most wonderful achievement of the White man was how he managed to turn Jesus Christ from being an Israelite into a European. The church, which was born in Jerusalem, has now become the White man's invention. The White man wrote all the stories and history about man and anything done by a White man is considered authentic even if it is bad or a lie.

Considering the few examples discussed above, the White man simply needs to be labeled as a born psychologist or a better visionary. For this, they own no apology since others could have chosen to do the same or similar. The White man's way of presenting facts and life is systematic and pretty, and therefore, captures the attention of humanity. The White man has become the role model for most people.

Unlike the White man, most of the great works done by the Black man have disappeared and no one talks about them much. The Black man knows about the White man's history more than his own history, though a lot was done by the Black man too.

The past glories and fame should not have disappeared, but instead, been improved upon. How can a people be great and then be poor after some time? What happened to their skills and abilities?

As the world is advancing, most African countries are still struggling to survive. The knowledge and achievements of most Black people were not pursued and developed. Instead, they disappeared from history and even when they are traced, they do not count for much and are irrelevant in today's world.

The modern generation is also hindered by the economic instabilities which discourage them from releasing their full potential. They are enticed by the White man's presentation of his package and they run for it. Most of the African thinkers contribute to the development of the western culture whereas Africa continues to fall.

The days where kings ruled over nations for decades, until their death, no longer exist. Eternal rule is no more a strategic leadership plan. It is known that wisdom is not in one man's head, therefore, after four to eight years in governance, a leader must allow another competent person to have access to leading the country. This is, however, not the case in many African countries.

When the African leaders taste power, they refuse to allow anyone the chance to lead because they think that the ability to lead has been given to them alone. They remain in power for many years until sometimes they are overthrown, killed or die of sickness. To maintain their control over the nation, they do everything by going the extra mile, even if they have to sell all the resources of the country to gain support.

In the thirst for power, Africans have fought among themselves, killing their own people and destroying the little development attained over the years. In Sierra Leone, Liberia, Rwanda and many other African countries, the people fought themselves, killing innocent people and destroying the nation based on very embarrassing concepts.

In Rwanda, the conflict that led to the bloody tribal war was little less than ridiculous. According to the movie **Hotel Rwanda**, the Rwandan people expected foreign aid to stop the fight, but nobody showed up and they were disappointed and embittered. The question is, why start a fight in the hope that someone else will intervene? The condition of Africa is well known. It is reckless, therefore, for any African nation to engage in any tribal or national war.

In Sierra Leone, the rebel fighters demonstrated irresponsible inhumane behavior that was breathtaking. They did not only kill innocent people but dismembered people for pleasure, leaving the victims disabled. They opened the wombs of pregnant women, still alive, and burnt people in their homes.

After the war, most of these rebels who did these horrible acts ran to Europe for help, forgetting what they had done in their own country. After destroying their own country, they looked for help from abroad. Some claim that the Westerners were behind the war, but I say that the Black people fought the fight, not the White man. When someone asks you to go and kill your mother, you have to ask the person to kill his mother to show you how to do it before deciding whether you want to kill your own mother or not. Therefore, if anyone says that the Europeans were behind the wars that occurred in Africa, then there must be evidence to show that that was the case.

Whether the Westerners were behind the wars or not, do the Africans not have brains to think and decide what is good for them?

Why should the Black man always blame others for something they should take responsibility for?

The fall of Africa is as the result of Africans who did not know the value of leadership but thought that the seat of government was for filthy lucre. As the nations sink in poverty, the leaders enjoy maximum protection and wealth. The citizens also live in such a way that contributes to the fall of the continent.

In Nigeria, many people have died due to armed robbery. Many more have been stripped of their possessions because innocent families were attacked and robbed of their possessions during the night and sometimes, in the day, by other Nigerians, making life unbearable. Almost every window in the houses in Ghana and Nigeria have been made burglar-proof to prevent thieves from entering.

People are killed just for mobile phones and watches and televisions. The life of a man is of lesser value than a mobile phone in Africa. Many have had their fingers and ears chopped off just to steal their mobile phones from them.

The African people complain of scant or no work as an excuse for the atrocities created. It is true that the unemployment rate is very high, and thus, many African youths and even the middle-aged adults run from their countries to the Western countries for jobs. At the same time, the Chinese and other people of non-African origin enter Africa, and see uncultivated opportunities, riches that have never been touched by anyone and they use the opportunities presented well.

The richness of a thing is in what it contributes or the value it adds to life and this applies to both humans and things.

Whenever an African President is sick, he flies abroad for medication because he does not trust the medical assistance in his own country. He knows that if he is not treated outside the country and left to be medicated in his own country, the chances are that he will die. If this be the case, then why subject your own citizens to sub-standard healthcare that is not good enough for you as the President? What stops the President from noticing the condition of the hospitals in the country and improving them? Does it mean that there are no doctors competent enough in Africa?

Another issue with Africans is that they dwell on past glories. The Africans or Black people must not dwell on the ancient success, but they must find their place in the modern developments which reflect the achievements of this present age. What some Black personalities did thousands of years back fulfilled the stories of that age. Likewise, those of this present age must demonstrate the skills and abilities needed to make history once again.

As much as past glories beautify history, the present situation of a thing is what counts. Once upon a time, I was rich but now I am poor; weigh that against once upon a time, I was poor but now I am rich. I believe the latter is better.

The Black man has taken too long in his struggle to fully arise and break away from his shackles. The majority of Black people live in extreme poverty which makes them vulnerable. Such vulnerability forces them to agree to anything they are offered. The Black man must arise and face the facts by accepting the challenge to do better. He did this in the ancient past and must be ready to do it again. Some of the achievements of certain wonderful Black individuals in various sectors of life indicate that, academically and practically, there is nothing wrong with the 'Black Man'.

"The Black man must arise and break away from binding shackles"

CHAPTER FIFTEEN

Black Education

In his book entitled **THE CHURCH, UNVEILING THE TRUTH**, Bishop Evans Antwi-Adjei, defined education as,

> *"The giving of information to train a person on a subject or field of interest for a proper performance or service in life".*

He also explained that, *"Education is a disciplinary method to enable a person to concentrate and acquire or improve their skills and abilities to properly use their talents and knowledge".*

Education, therefore, is a necessity for everyone living on this earth. Life itself is a great school and many who pay attention to it learn fast and understand how to live happily and progressively. Every group of people is responsible for their own education.

For example, every man is responsible for his own wife and children. It is unheard of and unexpected that you marry and think that another man will take care of your wife and children. If that happens, that man has the right to influence your family the way he wants. That is why it is necessary for every group of people to take their own education seriously.

Education has been one of the cultures of the Western countries. They took their time to positively educate and indoctrinate their people on what they want them to become in life and created different fields of learning to improve their quality of life. Education has catapulted the Western countries ahead of many others because they knew that educated people are reasonable people, people who contribute positively to their society.

Education shapes the character and attitudes of a person or people. Education influences people's behavior, speech and thoughts. How a child is educated informs his character which becomes his culture or tradition. That is why it is necessary for every group of people to properly educate their own people to pass on very appropriate and vital information to enrich the individual. Often, the educated aim high and want to perform as well as they can. When a person or people lose their educational values, they end up becoming what they are not because they learn things about other people which, most times, are not suitable for their own development.

As a student, the education I received in my country prepared my mind to live abroad because I learnt more about the Western culture than my own culture. I basically knew very little about my own country and my people as compared to the Western countries. I could not write or read my own language very well, but I was punished most times at school when I did not speak English.

My language was known as vernacular or primitive dialect whereas English was international. Many people lost interest in education because they found it hard to learn and speak the English language properly as they could not understand the vocabulary and the formation of the sentences. These people who dropped out of school were considered as illiterates because they could not speak English.

Until I travelled to Europe, I thought all the Westerners spoke English. I later discovered that each European country spoke their own language and were taught the same at school with English taken only as an option. Then I asked myself, why were we forced to learn another man's language? Why were we not taught in our own language since we understood this well?

I often marvel at how the Chinese and Japanese can write their own language although it is complex. These groups of people learnt their own language first even before considering any other language or they learnt it alongside other foreign languages. The learning of any other language is optional to many other people except the Black man. When a person learns by their own language, they can understand what they are taught well compared with when they learn using another man's language.

The Arabs speak their language and teach their people by the same. The English people speak their language and teach their children with the same language. Though they colonized many nations, they never used any of the languages of the people they colonized. Learning of others' language is, therefore, secondary. When the English people came to Ghana (West Africa), they introduced their language because that would make their work easier. Why should a few people who went to a country impose their own language on others or rather, why should people in a country yield to learning the language of others before their own?

Languages reflect and identify people. For example, when you hear a Black man speaking Japanese, it immediately sounds strange until it is explained that the Black man was born there or learnt the language. But when you hear a British man speak English, it sounds normal because that is his language and it identifies him.

Therefore, the education of a people using their own language is necessary. The English or European language spoken in most African countries brought about great limitation to their development because Africans are not English-speaking people; neither are they Europeans. Africans had to, and still must, learn and function with a language that does not identify them.

As a student, I had friends who were very intelligent but could not express themselves appropriately in English and were therefore mocked and ignored for it. Very intelligent people dropped out of school because they did not pass the English exams. Using English or other European language to teach the Black man infers that the native African languages are not good enough to be used for teaching the people. It also infers that no matter what the Black man knows, he must be made to learn and speak the English language or other European language to qualify his knowledge.

The White man is not responsible for the Black man's education because he has his own people to educate. The Black man is responsible for the education of his own people. Unfortunately, the educational system in Africa does not prepare the Black man to function in Africa. From nursery to the university, the Black man is prepared to hope for better job opportunities abroad. In his quest for a better life, the Black man sees the White man's education as the best for him, but he later finds out that he has lost his own identity.

When the Westerners came to Africa and introduced their culture and educational system, it seemed good at the initial stages, but it was just a superficial education because the Africans were molded through their teachings to function as it fit the White man's cultural demands. They did not prepare or teach the Africans anything extraordinary to enable them to develop themselves. It was not their responsibility. They taught the Africans what was beneficial to the White man's economy, including how to obey their rules and work for them. The educational system the White man introduced taught the Black man about the greatness and achievements of the Western countries.

Up until present day, there are African students who do not know what the name of their current President is, but they can tell you all the names of the leaders or leaders of the United States of America, Canada, Australia and Europe, including their ministers and their history. They are aware and have full or some knowledge of all the happenings in the Western countries and why they are developed, their challenges and solutions. However, they cannot figure out how to put food on their own table. They do not know how to help their own country but have the solutions to help the Western World.

The education of the African or Black people is the responsibility of the Black Man. The Black man knows the challenges of his people and the syllabuses that can stir their abilities to release their potential to function to the maximum. The Black man knows the language to communicate to his people that will facilitate their understanding to operate smartly.

Education is a necessity. Education boosts the knowledge and understanding of people, which also triggers their inner abilities and lets them use their brains to invent and create things beyond human imagination. When a person is educated wrongly, it blocks their functionality and causes them to render very little. Wrong education causes a people to function below average and makes them believe a lie about their personality. It makes them accept the opinion of others about them, even though such opinion may be fallacious.

Most Black people are wrongly educated, and they function exactly the way they were programmed, and this has placed great limitations on them. There are a lot of African graduates who do not know what to do in life after going through the stress of education because what they learnt at school cannot be applied in real life.

When the youth who are supposed to bring fresh ideas are blocked through wrong education, then the whole country is halted. The people suffer, and the country falls into debt because nobody can instigate what will bring a change. Amazingly, most African scholars do very well outside their countries. Their level of performance in the foreign societies becomes so high and they contribute a lot to make other countries better. The education many Blacks have had is simply not suited for their own country but for other countries and that is part of the root of the Black man's problem.

The Black man must not cast the responsibility of his proper education on the White man in any way, because, no matter what has transpired over the years, the Black man is not obligated to educate his people the way the White man wants. The Black man has the sole obligation to re-educate his people to encourage them to give their best to achieve life's purposes.

Wrong education sabotages innovations. When a group of people remains ignorant for a long time, they turn to attack those who have fresh ideas because it scares them to try anything new. That is why Africans must check their educational system and correct the things that are unnecessary because they are responsible for the education of their people. Black scholars must come together to craft proper educational programs to correct the old educational system that has crippled the abilities of the Black people. They must introduce productive syllabuses that would enable the Black man to think and function better. It is not the duty of the White man to design the educational life of the Black man because even if he does that, many vital things would still be omitted consciously or unconsciously and that would damage the thinking pattern of the Black man. Black men must rise up and acknowledge the value of proper and innovative education that would transform the lives of the Black people, whether in the Motherland or the diaspora.

Sadly, most African leaders, rich men and women, school their children abroad because they trust in Western education and deem it more appropriate than their national schools. There is no embitterment towards schooling abroad, but I believe that schools must be built for the Black man that are fit for purpose to match the standard of any school in the world with the required structures in place to help build the people to perform better.

Illiteracy is another issue regardless of the system of education used. Illiteracy must be seen as worse than any cancerous disease and anything that can be done to eliminate its trace from Black society must be treated with maximum dedication. Higher percentages of Africans are illiterate and very little care has been given to this dangerous determinant of health and progress.

It is sad to say that the educational system in Africa has been infested with corruption and the value of education is misunderstood. Teachers and professors compromise their work for money by not considering the brains they are damaging but focusing only on the money they can make. Instead of building the students, they break them by refusing to teach them with honesty. After many years spent in the educational system, due to strikes by teachers or failures of student or sometimes some other ridiculous reasons, most of these students finish school not knowing what to do because they did not learn anything. In many cases, the brains of students are tickled rather than exercised.

The Black Man must rise up and understand his value, his purpose, his history, his vision, his aim, his potential, skills and abilities to design proper patterns to educate his people for better performance in life.

"Is the Black man wrongly educated?"

CHAPTER SIXTEEN

The African Tradition

According to Merriam Webster's dictionary definition of the word "Tradition", it means;

> *"A way of thinking, behaving, or doing something that has been used by the people in a particular group, family, society, etc. for a long time"*

OR

> *"The stories, beliefs, etc., that have been part of the culture of a group of people for a long time".*

The dictionary breaks it down further by explaining that tradition -

1. **Is an inherited, established, or customary pattern of thought, action or behavior (as a religious practice or social custom)**
2. **A belief or story or a body of beliefs or stories relating to the past that are commonly accepted as historical though not verifiable**
3. **The handing down of information, beliefs, and customs by word of mouth or by example from one generation to another without written instruction.**

In other words, traditions are man-made beliefs passed on from generation to generation. If traditions are man-made beliefs or stories, it therefore means that errors can be made in their construction and transmission. For example, for a man to keep his family strictly under his control, he can invent a story that would bring his family under his authority, which, if not detected, could be practiced from generation to generation, thus making it tradition.

As beautiful as traditions may be, they can keep a people in bondage if the stories or beliefs that are practiced are considered sacred and amendments are forbidden. It must be noted that anything that is man-made can be corrected or improved on since human error is inevitable but if there is no room for analysis and changes, people can remain in obscurity for long periods of time which can affect their functionality and performance in life. Traditions, therefore, can be beautiful but destructive at the same time.

Every country is represented by their various traditions that distinguish them from one another. The traditions of some countries are so beautiful and attractive that it has become a world-wide tradition practiced by almost all people. For example, the celebration of Christmas with the pine tree decorated with lights and gifts is a Western tradition and it is practiced almost everywhere in the world, whereas some traditions are scary, sacred and secretive, something that can be termed the SSS traditions.

Some traditions involve the sacrifice of animals and sometimes, secretly demand humans as well. Some traditions forbid women's education or participation in any public affairs. Some traditions dictate circumcision in women to make them more acceptable to their husbands.

Most traditions around the world show why some people have developed and some have not. Some traditions keep people from thinking and analyzing the old stories and beliefs, whether they are beneficial to the present generation or not, whereas others allow people to stop or amend the old beliefs and stories to suit the present generation or current time.

Unless understood from the human point of view and altered, tradition structures human thinking regardless of how educated they are. Tradition makes people see the forefathers as infallible gods who have permanently defined the way of life.

If the Mercedes Benz of 50 years ago was not improved but was considered as the permanent irrevocable automobile for the Western market, it would have been erroneous and would have stagnated all the Mercedes Benz markets and remodeling that have been enjoyed for years. In the same vein, every man-made invention, creations, beliefs, culture, customs and stories can, and should be, changed or amended or remodeled to improve the standard of life of the people.

Every succeeding generation is wiser and more knowledgeable than the former. Therefore, stories and beliefs must be carefully criticized and analyzed by the latter, to avoid unpardonable errors. Traditions can seriously entangle people and cripple their pattern of thought and such will affect their potential and abilities.

The African continent is one of the continents which is riddled with traditions. Every nation and tribe have their own beliefs and stories passed on from generation to generation which are strictly irrevocable, no matter the negative effect they have had on people.

As poor as Africans might be, they are ready to die rather than revoke their traditions passed on to them. Africans consider their forefathers wiser and more intelligent than the present generation. For this reason, they consult them to seek for counsel and directions on how to progress and live in the present age. They believe wholeheartedly and follow without question the stories and beliefs passed on to them and without attempting to weigh the content of the information received. Any attempt to conceive the idea to investigate the traditions becomes an unpardonable sin.

How can a Neurosurgeon consult his great grandfather who did not go to school on how to operate on a patient? Yet, the great grandfather has laid down beliefs and stories that are controlling this Neurosurgeon. The very educated Africans are the ones fueling most of the horrible traditions that limit the people of Africa. Most of the African traditions have sabotaged the pattern of thought of the people because they are not permitted by the belief to think otherwise. The traditions affect every part of their lives, including their academic life.

Most of the documentaries shown on television and information on the internet about the African traditions show how beautiful the African traditions are, but the truth is, it might be beautiful in the eyes of the narrator because their film would bring them a lot of money by showing strange and controversial information.

As a very good example, the Mursi and Surma (Suri) women of Ethiopia put plates in their lip to beautify themselves and to look more attractive. The bigger the plate, the more dowries the father gets, which means that the beliefs of these people obligate the women to deform their own faces and it is seen as beauty. In Ghana, Nigeria and most parts in Africa, horrible tribal marks are drawn on the faces and bodies of people to differentiate them from other tribes. There are people whose faces are deformed as if they had fought with tigers, but these were the operations of traditional men. There are certain traditional practices in Africa that must be eliminated due to the damage it causes people. The fear of breaking the ancestral beliefs which are considered as sacred has prevented some people from daring to reason even if they suffer.

Among the Black people, there are some practices, not just in the Motherland but everywhere they are found, which are considered as traditions. These traditions do not yield wealth or progress. Instead, they produce limitations, hindrances and low performances in life. Traditions must be examined to know the cause and effect it brings on people. They must be analyzed to determine if they are to be continued or abandoned because they are man-made beliefs and stories. We must not forget that anything a person believes affects their pattern of thoughts, which goes on to interfere with their functionality and productivity in life. Therefore, Africans must examine themselves to know if what they believe has any negative consequences.

Traditions and Complicated Relationships

The Holy Bible, in the second chapter of Genesis verse 4, teaches,

"Therefore, a man shall leave his father and mother and be joined to his wife, and they shall become one flesh".

Practically, this is the marriage ordinances in almost all the cultures of the world except the African marriage which has an attachment. In the African marriage, the man basically does not leave his father and mother and neither does the woman because they literally carry all their family members into the marriage. This is to say, when an African man marries an African woman, he automatically marries the father, mother, Aunties, Uncles, brothers, sisters, nieces, nephews, cousins, grandparents and the family friends as well and he becomes responsible for them. His own family members also depend on him for support. His responsibility multiplies by infinity because approximately every nine months, a child is born into either family.

When the man is well to do, i.e., when the man is rich, the conflict between the two families increases because each one wants his attention. To save his soul from premature death, the African man must declare his inability to cater for his wife and children by his lifestyle which indicates poverty. He finds this more bearable than to incur insults from both families. When the families know that the man does not have money, it saves him from some undesirable pressures.

In Ghana, there are some tribes that practice that when a husband dies, his properties belong to his nephews instead of his wife and children because their tradition demands it so. The wife and children are denied access to their father's belongings if there was no **Will** written indicating their rights. The children become stranded if their mother cannot support them.

Other tribes have more difficult traditional practices that are breathtaking, and nobody dares to rise against these practices because they are sacred and irrevocable. Sometimes, the African man must support his nieces and nephews because his sister's husband cannot afford to take care of his own children, but the sister's husband has the strength to create new life every year.

Unlike the Western countries where giving birth is an individual choice, in Africa, it is obligatory. Whether the family has food to eat or not, it is a sacrosanct traditional obligation for the couple to produce children, as many as they can. There is no proper planning or vision, neither is there any pain in the heart of the parents to see numerous children running about without any proper education, food or sanitation.

A celebrated African bride is the one who has borne more children for her husband. She is considered a fruitful tree, a blessing and she is envied by all other women, even if she has no food to eat or food to give to her children. The priority of the African woman is to marry and give birth to as many children as she can because that would make her accepted by society and the man's family, otherwise, she will be regarded and treated as a witch. Women who do not have children are regarded as witches who eat their children in the spirit world instead of giving birth to them, and this is a common traditional belief in Africa. Families, friends and society fail to understand or reason that sometimes, the men may be the problem and not the women.

I spoke to a woman who came for counseling some years back and she told me that she wanted a child. I asked her if she had a husband and she answered no. Then I asked her if she worked and she said no. At this point, I was a little concerned. She explained that she had been looking for a child for quite some time but all her effort with her boyfriends led to nothing. She went on to say that she was aging, and that she wanted to give birth before she would be classified as a witch, barren and useless. I persuaded her that she first needed to put her life in order by securing a job and a house which were important for her life. I explained that it was only then that it would be sensible to engage in sound relationship to give birth. She looked at me and laughed and explained that she was not interested in securing a job or a house or husband because she did not need a husband to have a baby. She explained that all she needed was a man or anything that resembled a man to get her pregnant. She added that she was so desperate that she could even sleep with Satan to have a child. I was speechless. This is a typical African woman and her priority in life.

On national television in some of the Western countries, there are TV commercials that implore people to donate money to help African children because they are dying of hunger and infested with sicknesses, and most of them do not have shoes and dresses to go to school. Though this is very loving and caring, it is usually inadequate because it ignores what the African fathers and mothers think and how they perceive having many children and the importance they attribute to this.

In Uganda, a 39-year-old African woman had 44 children and lost 6, leaving her with 38 children. Though she had a rare condition that stimulated the conception of triplets and quadruplets, she still could have enjoyed her sexual life by using contraceptives to prevent pregnancy. At age 39, there are more chances that she could give birth again. In the Western countries, her state would be classified as abnormal and absurd but in Africa, she is celebrated as a queen because she is fruitful, in fact, very fruitful. Her poor state does not matter much, and the future of the kids is not a concern because she sees the children as a blessing.

In Nigeria, a man had 86 wives and had 185 children which attracted the press because it sounded like a fairy tale, but it was real. His wives and children were so proud of him. His beliefs permitted him to marry many wives and have many children to the point of absurdity. There are many untold stories in Africa concerning traditions, cultures and beliefs that need to be redefined if only to promote positive public health.

One of the major problems of the Black man is in the way he thinks and how he allows his beliefs to influence his behavior. The Black man's beliefs have influenced his thought pattern, which has also conditioned his performance. There are places in some parts of Africa that could be used as tourist attractions but rather, they are classified as sacred to the gods. In some local areas, the people are forbidden to go to the farms to work because the fetish priest says that the gods would be offended. An example is my own town. When I was young, whenever we visited our village or town, I noticed that no one went to the farm on Tuesdays because it was forbidden by the gods of the land. Law-breakers were punished. Such practice has been known to bring a whole community to a halt with ceased productivity.

No one dares to question the traditional practices because the stories and beliefs are untouchable. Individuals who chose to renew their minds on certain beliefs have attained some level of success that shows that the Black man also has the brain that is rich and skilled like any other human. If some Black people have overcome every limitation to become successful, then Africa must watch and follow their footsteps to amend some of the things that have crafted their way of thinking, to achieve a new perception.

"The Black man is limited by his traditions"

CHAPTER SEVENTEEN

The Black Man and Religion

Merriam Webster Dictionary defines religion as,

"The belief in a god or group of gods" OR

"An organized system of beliefs, ceremonies and rules used to worship a god or group of gods" OR

"An interest, a belief or an activity that is very important to a person or group" OR

"The service and worship of God or the supernatural; Commitment or devotion to religious faith or observances" OR

"A personal set or institutionalized system of religious attitudes, beliefs and practices. A cause, principle or system of beliefs held to with ardor and faith".

Religion, therefore, is a very powerful thing because one way or the other, all the people in the world are religious. Everybody has something they believe in. Like tradition, religion has great control over people. Religion is more powerful than tradition because tradition deals with the beliefs of a people from a specific place whereas the same religion can be practiced by groups of people anywhere in the world.

The world is paying a huge price to maintain peace among men because of their different religious practices. Many religions claim that their religion is the right way, and this has created serious hatred among men. Most of the wars that had been fought in this world can be classified as religious wars, and war has become more dangerous in this present age.

Anything a person believes controls their minds and their functionality. We must understand that the god or gods people believe in also have their rules and conditions and they want their subordinates to follow their instructions and practice their ordinances with all dedication. This can cause a person to forsake their purpose and desires, plans and hopes, developments and potential to satisfy their religion.

Many or all religions do not only require the people to be obedient to their rules and precepts but have reserved punishment for those who refuse to obey the rules of the gods. The fear of punishment by these gods can cause people to totally abandon their skills, abilities and purpose to avoid the anger of their gods.

Religion, therefore, is a powerful controlling weapon. There are those who can do anything in the name of religion, including killing others if the religion demands so. Many families have been torn apart because of religion and many nations have been bound and turned to hate other nations because of religion. There are individuals who are afraid to talk or express themselves, either privately or publicly, because they are afraid of what religious people may do to them. A husband can betray a wife and vice versa if one of them discovers that the other had a different mindset against their religion, because religion honors informants and condemns traitors.

Religion produces great fear and it cripples a person physically and mentally. Those who refuse to be part of any religion are sometimes right because at least they can use their own mind to decide what they want or like. Religious people, most times, condemn those who do not get themselves involved in any religious practice, yet they envy their progress and achievements and desire to have what they produce.

Believing in something or someone is not bad, it is part of life. There are many witnesses that man is not alone in the universe and scientists affirm that there are invisible beings that invade our planet daily, but the irony is that, when the desire of a god or gods condition, and sabotage, the strength and abilities of the people, then it becomes a problem. A god or belief that causes division among men and demands that the worshippers or subordinates abandon everything and dedicate their lives only to do their will is a problem.

If everyone is seated at home just to worship a god, then who will go to the farm to grow crops? Who will build the houses for people to have shelter? Who will construct roads and bridges, cities, hospitals, supermarkets, make the dresses and shoes, or build the planes and ships and trains and cars and all the things that have contributed to aid humanity?

To believe in a god is not the problem, but the application of the requests of that god is the problem. Everybody has the right to believe or not to believe in something, whether seen or unseen, but when what a person believes becomes a dictatorial concept, that obligates people to function and think in such a way that it demands killing of others, then that god or belief must be analyzed properly.

Religion must not be given the right to destroy the peace among men, but it must be practiced with common sense, either publicly or privately, to enhance love. No religion must become a threat to people or obligate people to accept it by force, but engagement in and with religion must be a free choice an individual makes after hearing and analyzing the contents of its message.

As much as the belief of an individual or a people cannot be stopped, the authorities of every nation still have the mandate to maintain order and declare its religious belief/s. For example, there are nations that are known as Christian nations, whereas some are Islamic nations and some are Buddhist nations, and so on. These nations have declared their religious beliefs and they do not have to promote any religious chaos, controversies and unstableness. When any religious person enters any nation that has defined their belief, that individual or people must respect the nation's belief and practice theirs quietly without disturbances and the natives of that nation must not be hindered from believing in what they think is right or would help and benefit them.

This has, however, not been the case, especially as religion has always won the front seat in the human mind. Religion is a great dictator, a ruler without mercy, a perverse judge and a confiscator of human rights. Religion is never satisfied of its atrocities of turning people against each other and pushing people to commit inhumane acts. Napoleon Bonaparte, a French military and political leader once said,

"Religion is what keeps the poor from murdering the rich".

If every religious person could separate their soul from the demands of their religion and reason as normal humans, I believe the power and control religion has on humans would be broken. The human brain is a great gift and a reservoir of potential, but religion has seized the brain of most people and has made them bound and impoverished. Most humans are only active when it comes to religious duties.

Africans had their own religious beliefs which they practiced, until the Europeans brought the gospel of Jesus Christ to them. Christianity had been in Africa for a long time before this, but the Europeans came to Africa to preach about Jesus Christ and many other things. They saw the need to colonize every African nation they travelled to because they believed that Africa must be led by people who were more enlightened, which was a mistake.

Their duty was to preach the gospel but not to rule over the people, but their actions later made the gospel not to be credible because the same people who taught them about God and love, were the same people who took over their land to rule them. The Africans now needed permission from the gospel carriers to do anything in their own land.

Regardless, the gospel still made its way into the minds and hearts of many Africans and they started to practice this new belief. This new belief became a fundamental belief of most African nations, but the problem was the practice of this belief. Tradition had played a great role in delaying the African, and now, religion has also invaded the Black society.

The Christian belief, per se, is a great religion because of the message it carries and the evidence that supports the belief. However, there have been many interpretations of the Bible which has divided Christians into many groups and subgroups and this has affected the Black man immensely. When an African believes in something, most especially when it comes to spiritual things, he becomes sold and gives his reasoning power to the thing and the thing begins to dictate and control everything about him. In many senses, religion has held the African slave again.

Whilst a few people are truly teaching the doctrine of Jesus Christ as indicated in the bible, millions of other people have sprung up using the Bible to entangle others. People who do not have any idea about what the Bible says, untrained and uneducated people, have used the Bible to stop millions of people from reasoning. Most Black Christians believe that, after praying, they must sit down doing nothing and their God will bring them food to eat as He gave to the people of Israel thousands of years ago when they left Egypt.

In Africa, many people sit in the church from morning until evening to pray for months and they believe that their problems could be solved without improving themselves through education and developing their skills. Even the Bible says that,

Faith without works is dead

Yet, the African Christian has his own interpretation about faith.

The dangers of religion to Africa are that doctrines are taught by people who are not educated theologically, although they claim that they are mandated by God and place bondage on the people. Today, because of how technology has advanced, information travels very quickly, whether good or bad, and desperate people are caught in the net of deception and entangled by incorrect information concerning Christianity.

The African is not only dealing with traditional limitations, but religious limitations. Some of the church practices indicate how ignorant most Black people are. For example, a pastor of a church claimed that God told him to give dead rats to people to eat and he did it and the followers ate rats with joy saying that it tasted like biscuit. Another asked the people to eat grass and the people ate grass like cows and they rejoiced.

Other pastors claimed that to wash away bad luck from their congregants, they had to bathe them naked by the riverside and they did that. Due to the level of illiteracy in Africa, tradition and religion are used by unscrupulous people to immerse the people into deeper bondage. People are ready to go every mile to satisfy their traditional and religious beliefs.

Today, in Africa, establishing churches is in great demand because most people have taken this as a job that can fetch a lot of money. Everywhere Black people are gathered, there are churches of all sorts to ensnare the people all the more.

I believe in God and I am a Christian. I am a preacher and have been a leader for many years, but I feel sorry to see what Christianity is doing to Black people, especially those on the African continent. The level of bondage is high, and the deception in the practice of Christianity is sometimes disgusting. Many people are in bondage which has affected their thinking capacity.

Of all the many things that have held Africa bound, tradition and religion play the major role. Black people are very intelligent but when they believe something, most especially concerning the supernatural, they are ready to sacrifice their own development and submit all their skills and abilities to appease their beliefs and this has halted them from advancing.

There are a lot of African scholars, inventors, scientists, architects, engineers, pilots, and many others who have proved to the world that there is absolutely nothing wrong with the Black man, but what a person believes is very important because it goes a long way to affect their abilities.

Another dimension to this is the self-image that people have. Many people believe that they are ugly-looking, and they behave likewise. They feel inferior towards others and are intimidated and shy all the time.

Some believe they are not intelligent because they cannot understand a subject. Some believe they are poor and can never have money and some even believe they will not live long in life. What people believe in, unless changed, will condition and control their potential. Though what people believe others think of them may influence them, what they believe about themselves has greater power. Many Black people have this feeling of inferiority, usually informed by limited material wealth. Such perception of self is usually what pushes them to seek for a solution and this is what leads them to these many churches and Christian houses as well as traditional spiritual shrines that unfortunately damages their self-perception more in the long run. Black people must change the way they think because there is a great deal of positive evidence from other Black men and women who have done exceedingly great things in the past and in our time.

"The Black man is bounded by religiosity not spirituality"

CHAPTER EIGHTEEN

Breaking The Limitations

Every successful person had to search within themselves to find who they really were, why they were born, why they were on this planet and what should be their contribution to help the human race.

The greatest gift that man possesses is the brain. Therefore, the moment the brain is programmed wrongly, it affects everything about him. Whatever we give attention to, gives us direction and whatever we believe in, condition us. Therefore, it is very necessary to believe in oneself and guard the brain from incorrect information. Everyone must understand their uniqueness and value to avoid someone else polluting their brain.

The people who understand the power of the brain have advantage over those who do not. Anyone who eventually discovers the potential embedded in their brain become powerful and successful just by understanding what the capabilities of their brain are.

The American Educationist Jane Elliot said,

"There is no superior or inferior race or different races, but we have only one race and that is the human race".

All men are equal no matter their physical appearance. The knowledge of the capabilities of the brain and its appropriate usage can make men productive. Life is full of challenges and surprises, and those who confront these become successful.

It is not enough to be intelligent; a person must learn also to be smart and not to entangle themselves in things that would hinder them from developing their potential. Procrastination, laziness, excuses, fear, an inferiority complex, irresponsibility and accusations (the list is endless) have caused many people to remain in their shell and never step out to influence their world.

Most Black people are full of excuses and accusations and they are lazy and irresponsible. Many Black people also think that their poor condition is justifiable through slavery and exploitation but there are some Black men and women from even worse backgrounds with very hard life experiences who did not allow their situation and the social conditions to stop them. These people paid every price life demanded of them to become very successful. They did this because they looked at the potential and abilities within themselves rather than the conditions around them.

Take the Japanese, for example. The Japanese are hardworking people who developed their country by themselves through sacrifices. We often hear of the country going through numerous earthquakes, which should be limiting them, but the Japanese have built their country to resist these earthquakes and have provided their people with the best technology to survive it. They do not depend on anybody.

Dubai has shocked the world by its recent development. The resources of its country have been channeled to do something that makes the people proud. Many people travel to Dubai for business and for work. Countries like Singapore, China and South Korea also do their best to give their people a better life.

The minerals and oil extracted from the African soil should have made Africa the richest and most developed continent in the world, but evidently, it is the poorest. How can a continent be so rich and the people so poor?

How can a person have enough food in his house, yet die of hunger? It is either that the person does not know how to cook or is very lazy. Africa is wealthy, yet her people are entrapped in poverty. This suggests that it is either that the people do not know the value of the wealth they have or that they are lazy, but the more plausible explanation is connected to their pattern of thought.

The knowledge about Africa's wealth and the state of her people has made the world suspicious about the functionality of Africans.

Many people think that the Black man is unintelligent, but one need not wonder why they think so. The success of some Black people has proven this conception of lack of intelligence as wrong and revealed simply that the Black man has misplaced priorities.

The Black man must strive to break all limitations placed on him and it must start with a renewed pattern of thought. The next section of this book gives examples of some Black people who renewed their thoughts and thus were able to break the limitations.

"The Black man is not unintelligent but
has misplaced priorities"

The Queen of All Media

In January of 1954, the media goddess **OPRAH WINFREY** was born to a single mother in Mississippi in the United States of America. These were very hard days for Black people in America because of the high level of racism openly practiced against them in the country. Oprah Winfrey was born to a poor family and she had a very difficult child-hood. According to her story, she was molested several times and had a baby at age 14 although the child did not survive.

She was not favored by the law nor was she treated as a queen. Her treatment was not different to what other Black people experienced in the country. Her family was poor like most Black families and she was not exempt from the Jim Crow laws.

- Jim Crow was a pejorative expression meaning Negro. Jim Crow laws were state and local laws that enforced racial segregation in the southern United States.

Oprah narrated her story by saying how influential and inspirational her grandmother was to her, teaching her at a very young age to read and recite.

Due to the occupation of the grandmother, her good heart and her perception about the Black man's limited chances in the country made her constantly suggest to Oprah that she should learn her occupation to enable her to become a good housemaid in the future. Oprah was taught and prepared to be a housemaid simply because her grandmother could not figure out what else a Black woman could do in a country that had drawn its stand against the 'Black Man'.

However, Oprah had a different opinion of herself, and, as much as she loved her grandmother, she did not see herself cleaning people's rooms and cooking for them but believed that one day, she would be speaking to people to make her living.

Believing was one thing but fulfilling her dream in a country that everybody knew had very little chances for a Black man never mind a Black woman, was another. The chances that a Black male had were very few, and a Black woman had none. This reality alone could have scared young Oprah Winfrey from pursuing her dream.

Like every other dream, it did not happen just by hoping or expecting it to drop from the blue skies, but it took self-discipline, hard work, determination, education, sacrifices, patience, and a renewed mind to accomplish it and Oprah Winfrey was determined to pay the price. The journey to her present position in life was not very pleasant but nothing could stop her; not even the color of her skin, which was a great hindrance in her time.

Oprah Winfrey worked very hard and demonstrated a higher level of wisdom, skills and abilities in her field of operation, and gradually, her hard work started to pay back. For 25 years, the **OPRAY WINFREY SHOW** was the most-watched and leading program in the country and around the world.

Today, she is the Chairwoman and chief executive officer (CEO) of Harpo Productions, and the Chairwoman, CEO and chief commercial officer (CCO) of the OPRAH WINFREY NETWORK (OWN). She is an actress, an author and a philanthropist. She is one of the most influential women that lives on the planet. In 2013, the President of the United States of America, Barrack Obama, awarded her the Presidential Medal of Freedom and an Honorary Doctorate Degree from Duke and Harvard Universities. In 2018, Oprah Winfrey was the first African American woman to receive the Cecil B. DeMille Award, an Honorary Golden Globe Award bestowed by the Hollywood Foreign Press Association for "outstanding contributions to the world of entertainment".

Without controversy, Oprah Winfrey is the richest Black woman in the United States of America according to Forbes' rating in 2017, born into poverty but risen into riches. Her unbeatable ability to communicate, her intelligence, her wisdom and knowledge have made her one of the most influential women on the globe.

Oprah Winfrey is an example of living proof to all Black people that there is nothing wrong with the brain of the Black man, but in all things, the pattern of thought, the way of life, hard work, sacrifices, determination and more, will always be the yardstick by which a man's success will be determined.

The Daughters of Hope

African women suffer a lot due to the masculine traditions practiced everywhere.

African women, most times, are not allowed to go to school because the fathers believe that it is of no use. They are prepared, from their infancy, for marriage and are only taught how to please their husbands through submission and servitude. An African lady's greatest desire is to make her husband happy by cooking good and delicious food for him and entertaining his friends whenever they visit. Her greatest achievement is to give birth to as many children as possible to prove her usefulness as a fruitful wife. Her failure to give birth draws the attention of the community against her as a witch and draws wrath from her husband as she is considered a disgrace.

All African men, by tradition, believe that they are fertile and have no problem fathering children. Therefore, if a woman is not able to give birth, the fault is only hers and she can be divorced for that reason or it could give reason for the man to marry other women.

Under no circumstances must a woman be richer than her husband or be more famous than him. It is the woman who bears a man's name but not the man who bears a woman's name according to most African traditions. Therefore, the woman must not be popular, famous or richer than her husband. These traditional beliefs present challenges for African women and places limitation on them.

The African woman is more or less a slave to her husband. She is responsible for all the domestic work in the house and must satisfy the man very well in bed at night too, otherwise, she is classified as a bad wife. She literally carries the entire load in the family. If it happens that she has a job, she must give her money to her husband because he is the head of the house and if the man does not work, it is her obligation to support him and make sure he is happy because that is how a good wife must behave.

For these reasons, many African women are not able to rise to do anything that would offend their husbands or families because of the strict traditions. Most African women are limited to selling some small commodities in the daily markets just to support the family because they are afraid to expand their skills and abilities due to the limitations placed on them by tradition. At least, this was how it was until recently.

Very talented, skilled, knowledgeable, wise African women were not allowed by the masculine traditions to contribute to the daily decisions of the families, let alone the communities and the nations and this has been one of the greatest mistakes of the African people.

In the land where women's rights were limited, where women were only to be found useful in the kitchen and bedroom, where women were, and are still considered as less important, Folorunso Alakija was born to a Nigerian family in 1951. Folorunso Alakija is a personality of hope to Africa and all African women around the globe about the potential women have to deliver the Motherland from her shame. It is not by mistake that the African continent is known as the Motherland and not the Man Land. The men have fought and resisted the progress of Africa by restricting the women from demonstrating their skills and potential to deliver the families and the nations as a whole.

As a Nigerian business woman involved in fashion, oil and the printing industries, Folorunso Alakija has fought untold battles, threats and offenses from intimidating men to silence the egoistic attitudes of the African man by demonstrating her ability to navigate through the business world. Her wisdom and success, self-control and confidence, determination and hard work have helped her to rise above all limitations.

As a female billionaire and the group managing director of the Rose of Sharon Group (printing and promotions company), she has, by her leadership abilities and the proper control of wealth, outlined the future of Africa. Folorunso Alakija's outstanding success exposes the untapped treasures hidden in the African woman. The fears, intimidations, advance education and traditions could not act as a barrier against her beliefs, but through hard work, vision and purpose in life, she stands amongst the richest and most influential women in the world. Her greatest achievement is the new picture she has drawn of Black people and the hope given to all African women. As a business woman, Forbes (2017) ranks her as the richest woman in Nigeria with an estimated net worth of $2.1 billion. Forbes still rates her as the 87th most powerful woman in the world.

There are no excuses for Black women, either in America or Jamaica, the Caribbean Islands, Haiti, South America or in the Motherland. Folorunso Alakija and many others have proved that there is nothing wrong with the Black man except his own pattern of thought, determination, sacrifices and hard work, which were not positively utilized, hence the limitations observed. The story of Africa has been re-written by people like Maya Angelou, Folorunso Alakija, Isabel de Santos, Oprah Winfrey, Sheila Crump Johnson, Hajia Bola Shagaya, and many more, who have understood their worth and potential to affect our world.

The "God" of Hollywood

Nothing comes easy in this life and every successful person has a story. Hard work pays and poverty is the reward for an idle soul. The rich get richer because they think and behave rich, while the poor get poorer because they also think and behave poor. The only bridges between the rich and the poor are determination, discipline, pattern of thought and hard work.

Just like the late reggae singer Peter Tosh said,

"Everybody wants to go to heaven, but no one wants to die".

Everybody wants to be rich but not all want to pay the price. People have always wanted the shortest way to make money by sleeping on their beds and just wishing to get rich. They then accuse the rich for taking everything.

Have you ever wondered why one person could be so rich and millions of others dwell in poverty? Why some people have enough for their dogs, whiles families go to bed hungry and why one person could own hundreds of houses while many sleep on the streets? It is truly amazing, but we must understand that wherever a person lives, the principles for success and poverty work without failure and anyone who applies them gets the same results.

One of the most educative movies I ever enjoyed watching was the **Pursuit of Happiness** starring **Will Smith**. Admittedly and without shame, I watched this film several times and any time I watched it, it brought tears to my eyes because it showed how hard work pays. Sometimes, a man must admit his laziness and step out of his comfort zone, and through hard-work and sacrifices, pursue his purpose in life.

In June 1st of 1937, Morgan Freeman was born in Memphis, Tennessee. The date of his birth indicates a very hard period for the Black Americans. He had every reason to complain and lament like every other Black man in America because the times were very unfavorable for the Black man. Morgan discovered his abilities quickly at an early age and participated in some competitions brilliantly.

Life challenges led him into the United States' Air Force where he served as an Automatic Tracking repairman and rose to the rank of Airman 1st Class. He moved to California where he started to pursue his dreams. He did certain unpleasant jobs to sustain himself, but he knew what he wanted in life. He never allowed anything to stop him but worked very hard to improve himself. Morgan Freeman won an Academy Award in 2005 and other awards for his outstanding performances as an actor. His unique voice is loved by many people and he has acted in many films.

He is one of the actors most loved and respected in Hollywood. Normally in movies, the personality of God is represented by a voice, but in the movie **Bruce Almighty,** Morgan Freeman dared to be God and made us able to see God, a role that would, in ordinary circumstances, be assigned to a White man, because who expected God to be a Black Man? His outstanding performance could not be overlooked. Morgan Freeman came down again from heaven as God to give another assignment to Evan in the movie, **Evan Almighty.**

The uniqueness of Morgan Freeman is revealed by the way he thinks. In one of his interviews, he said, "I am not an African, I am an American". He is not a Black American but an American and rightly so. Have you ever heard people saying, 'I am British American' or 'Dutch American'? No, they all call themselves Americans. Why, therefore, should Black people identify themselves as African Americans?

Morgan Freeman is firm in his convictions and I believe his strong will and wisdom has won him more respect as a man and as a great actor. In an interview, Morgan Freeman said, *"Discipline, humility and hard work are very important keys to success. He also said that a man must hold on to his principles".*

All the activities Morgan Freeman is involved in, which he conducts extraordinarily, show how great he is. Born in the era of extreme racism and injustice, he made up his mind to pursue his dreams through hard work, humility and discipline. These are principles of success which every Black man must apply.

At his present age, he is still a highly paid and active actor because he is the best at what he does. He could have complained and refused to do anything and become bitter due to all the injustices he saw around him, but he knew that the best way to help was to make his own life meaningful. He knew that to help, his life must present as an example to others.

Morgan Freeman is an icon in the movie industry and a personality of hope to people in America and around the globe. He has proved to all the Black men that nothing is impossible if only the principles of success are applied. We also have, as examples of great actors and actresses, personalities such as Sydney Poitier, Denzel Washington, Eddy Murphy, Will Smith, Samuel L Jackson, Danny Glover, Whoopi Goldberg and many more who have proved through their performances that the Black man has no excuse not to break the limits. The Black man has everything it takes to show his abilities, wisdom and knowledge. There is basically nothing wrong with the Black man, as indicated in almost every chapter of this book, except his own pattern of thought.

Nothing is Impossible

The dream of every young man in Africa is to travel and stay abroad. They believe that life abroad or in the Western countries is better and more promising than in their own country of birth. The Western countries seem to offer many opportunities to people of the Third World countries, including more employment and a better standard of living. Foreigners also enjoy the many facilities available which are scarcely seen in their own countries.

Some African men and women queue around western embassies from morning till evening in the search for permit visas, whereas the majority find other means to enter Europe. There is practically nothing good seen by most African young people in their own country; nothing to appeal to them to work hard unless it is to travel abroad.

A very small percentage of African people who have chosen to remain in their own countries believe that if the same principle practiced abroad was implemented in Africa, the same results would be attained. The majority of Africans who dwell on the land do so because they have no choice. Given the choice, many would leave Africa for European countries or others, anywhere except countries in Africa. There are many Africans who have travelled to other Third World countries under false hope, believing that every other country is better than Africa and, in those countries, if they work hard, they would succeed. Many leave Africa believing and ready to do any job to earn money. Most of the jobs Africans engage with in other countries are jobs they would not do in their own countries.

On this same African Continent which almost everybody wants to escape from, was born the great leader, Bishop David Oyedepo. On the 27th of September 1954, the township of Osogbo in Nigeria received the arrival of this great man. There was nothing extraordinary about his birth. He was born just like any other Nigerian. With the different religious beliefs of his parents, he was blessed to have his grandmother who trained him to pray and serve God properly, his grandmother being a born-again Christian. He studied architecture and worked briefly but the strong burden he felt in his heart about what God wanted him to do led him to dedicate his life to missionary work. He started to preach and teach people about faith in God and trust in His word.

He taught his congregation that nothing is impossible if you put your trust in God. At one time, he was a laughing stock because he spoke about what his God could do, but he had no physical evidence to prove it. However, he kept telling people about it and teaching them that God can help them achieve great things.

In no time, the evidence of his teachings started to manifest, and people began to see that, with God, all things are possible and whenever the principles of success are applied, it produces the same positive results.

Bishop David Oyedepo chose to remain in Africa and preach the gospel of Jesus Christ, demonstrating to all Africans that nothing is impossible if you implement the principles of success. He has influenced greatly, by his faith-based messages, the entire church of Jesus Christ. Many people have received education on how to be successful in life by following his teachings.

Though he is classified as the wealthiest preacher in Nigeria, the impact he has made is not by the wealth he possesses but by the lives he has affected and changed through his teaching. His church auditorium is one of the biggest in the entire world, seating 50,000 people at a time. Recently, he launched his vision of building a bigger auditorium that can seat 100,000 people at a time and this is in progress. He built the 50,000-seat auditorium in 12 months, debt-free, on a 2.1km square facility known as Canaanland.

He owns several schools, universities, banks and residential buildings built to serve communities, as well as the job opportunities he has offered to thousands of people. There are many other things this great leader has done with his gifts, faith, abilities, determination and wisdom that cannot be overlooked.

It takes a great leader to manage such an amount of wealth and number of people without any problem and it takes a high level of wisdom to keep increasing the wealth. Apart from Bishop David Oyedepo being a man of Faith, he has worked very hard to break all limitations around him to obtain such incredible results in Africa without any help from any organization or society abroad. In most of his messages, he keeps repeating that there is nothing done in the Western countries that cannot be done in Africa if only the principles of success are applied.

Bishop Oyedepo must not just be regarded as a man of Faith who has attained great success in life, but as a Black man who, through wisdom, knowledge, understanding, hard work, determination, discipline, perseverance, sacrifices and education, has demonstrated that there is nothing wrong with the Black man except his pattern of thought.

Bishop Oyedepo's achievements are ever-increasing because he has understood the principles that bring success. He is a highly intelligent man and principled in his endeavors.

Other great men like Bishop Tudor Bismark, Dr. Mensah Otabil, Dr. Matthew Ashimolowo, Bishop TD Jakes, Dr. Creflo Dollar and many more are Sons of the Common Faith in Jesus Christ who are changing the world through their messages and lifestyle, indicating that the Black man has no excuse not to rise and think, whether in the secular or missionary field because there is nothing wrong with him.

If Bishop David Oyedepo can rise to that level of achievement and performance in Africa without any help from foreign missions or organizations, then the African leaders have no excuse not to bring their nations out of poverty. Every Black man in his own field of work must demonstrate some level of excellence and success. There is evidence from both Black men and women who have, and continue to change, the story concerning the conception about the supposed unintelligent Black man, through their performances and achievements.

The Man of War

In 1957, on the 6th of March, Dr. Kwame Nkrumah and his team brought independence to Ghana from their Colonial Masters. Ghana was in great joy because, finally, they could decide on their own how to run the country without permission from their Colonial Masters. Dr. Kwame Nkrumah revealed his plan concerning the development of Ghana, which was excellent.

The Ghanaians' hopes and expectations were sky-high because they thought that everything would happen like magic without hard work, sacrifices, determination, and discipline, etc. The pressure fell on Dr. Kwame Nkrumah because he was seen by the people as the savior and there was no room for mistakes or failure.

Two months later, on the 12th of May 1957, the cry of a new-born baby was heard on the soil of Ghana announcing the arrival of Archbishop Nicholas Duncan-Williams, to a single parent. In an interview, Duncan-Williams narrated the complications surrounding his birth and the risk of death whenever he was sick.

His upbringing was not very pleasant for the mother because he became a difficult child who refused to go to school due to issues that harassed his mind. He learnt to survive on the streets by doing all kinds of things.

At age 16, he knew his biological father from the courtroom where, due to the situation around him, he was forced to choose to stay with him otherwise the alternative would have complicated his life all the more. In an interview, he told how he met his father for the first time in the courtroom and the option to stay with his father was the only opportunity he had to escape punishment. Then he learnt that his father had 43 other children.

He admitted that, due to the negative things he was told about his father, he had difficulties relating with him and this also contributed to the many wrong decisions he made as a young man. He asked himself a lot of questions about what he could do to find solutions for his life. He went about asking for help from mediums and Spiritualists regarding his difficulties. One day, he heard a voice which gave him a direction to light a candle and place his right hand on the fire without removing it, which he did. He narrated in an interview that he was over-powered by an unknown negative force which made him keep his hand on the fire until three of his fingers were burnt and melted away, when finally, he was rescued. His deformation was procured through the search for mental and social freedom.

Through this experience, he met some people who introduced him to the Gospel of Jesus Christ and he later accepted the call to preach the gospel. He was now faced with the challenge of education because he had not actually received much, and he could not read or write. He therefore decided to improve his life by re-educating himself and learnt to write with his left hand because of the incident that happened to his right-hand fingers.

Archbishop Nicholas Duncan-Williams waged his war through prayer to pioneer the Christian Charismatic Movement in Ghana, challenging the youth to serve God. From the streets of Accra to the Corridors of Power, the Archbishop demonstrated incredible leadership skill and potential which now echo in the lives of many Christians in Ghana, Africa and the world at large.

He is known all over the world as the Apostle of Strategic Prayer. Many have been his challenges over the years, but he has always waged his war through them all. He was named recently by the New African Magazine as one of the 100 most influential Africans in 2017. He became the first non-American to lead the prayer for the incoming President and Vice-President of the United States of America during the inauguration in 2016.

He is highly respected and honored among the Preachers of the Gospel in the entire world because of his insight about spiritual issues as concerning nations, families and individuals. Over the years, he has demonstrated higher levels of wisdom, knowledge and incredible understanding about Christianity. His preaching has enabled most young people to acquire instruction on how to serve God and live a successful life.

The life of Archbishop Nicholas Duncan-Williams is a great challenge for all Black people everywhere. His life simply reiterates that there are no excuses for poverty and unsuccessfulness. His life reveals that no matter the conditions, if a person is determined and works to change their pattern of thoughts to pursue excellence, nothing can stop them. Archbishop Duncan-Williams broke all limitations and decided, through discipline and determination, to turn his life around.

There are numerous other examples of Black men and women who have done great things. Their stories are not within the remit of this book. The purpose of this chapter was to bring to light the fact that the conception about the unintelligent Black man is only a conception that is untrue, and that Black men and women can break every limitation by applying success principles which every successful person in this world has applied.

The Black Man must arise and break all limitations
around him.

CHAPTER NINETEEN

No More Excuses

Whether concerning the slave trade or the Colonial rule and exploitation of Black people and Africa, which has caused the Black man to think that he needs the entire world to apologize to him and favor him in all things, the Black man must wake up and know that there are, and should be, no more excuses.

Slavery is no more an excuse for Black people not to educate themselves and improve their lives; neither should the Colonial rule be used as an excuse to support the hardship in Africa. These conceptions have negatively conditioned the minds of Black people over the years and have also poisoned the minds of young Black people from generation to generation.

Most Black people today still behave as if the slave trade continues and many more have refused to improve their lives because of this. The issue is hard to talk about because any attempt to address this problem makes most Black people think that someone is negating the evidence and facts about the injustices committed against the Black man, most especially in the United States of America and South Africa, but that cannot stop someone from educating themselves to have better chances to change laws and conditions that do not favor the Black man.

The way to fight against injustice is not by demonstrating on the streets but by being a part of the decision-making board to implement laws and measures that protect everyone. The way to fight against betrayal is to become successful in whatever you do. The way to fight offenses is to be happy every day. The way to fight racism is to be productive and excellent in everything. The way to fight poverty is to be rich sustainably. The way to have civil rights is to be part of the political powers. If a person does not know how to drive a car and must be driven by others all the time, then they would have to bear the driving conditions offered them, whether good or bad.

Even in the Western countries, it is not everybody that is successful or living well. The Western countries also have homeless people and unemployed people who find it hard to make a living. There are criminals whose residences are the prisons and those who do not understand what life is all about. The only fortunate thing for these people is that they are born into countries that are developed, where structures are in place to allow decent living even in the face of poverty, imprisonment and homelessness.

Coming from a poor family or country is not an excuse; not having parents is not an excuse; being born Black is not an excuse; not having money is not an excuse, and neither is not having formal education. No condition is permanent unless it is permitted to become so. When a person is determined, they can change their situation and live better. Where there is hard work, determination, discipline, sacrifices and striving, there is breakthrough.

People who have broken the limits in life and have changed their unfavorable conditions simply refused to entertain excuses. Rather than entertaining excuses, they focused on their dreams and paid the price through sacrifices to obtain their desired results. Sometimes, those who have attained some level of achievement are considered as people who were chosen by divinity before the foundations of the earth to be rich and influential, but this is not the case. These people worked hard to be where they are.

Excuses have been the number one cause of many poor people and in dealing with excuses, King Solomon wrote, in the book of Proverbs chapter 22 verse 13, that,

"The lazy man is full of excuses; I can't go to work, he says; if I go outside, I might meet a lion in the streets and be killed".

Proverbs 10 and verse 4 says,

"A slack hand causes poverty, but the hand of the diligent makes rich".

Proverbs 13 verse 4 says,

"The soul of the sluggard craves and gets nothing, while the soul of the diligent is richly supplied".

And Proverbs 6 verses 6 to 11 reads,

"Go to the ant, O sluggard; consider her ways, and be wise. Without having any chief, officer or ruler, she prepares her bread in summer and gathers her food in harvest. How long will you lie there, O sluggard? When will you arise from your sleep? A little sleep, a little slumber, a little folding of the hands to rest, and poverty will come upon you like a robber, and want like an armed man".

There are many other proverbs in the Bible citing excuses as the reason for poverty and dissatisfaction in life.

From his Proverbs, King Solomon gives us some of the reasons why people become poor or remain poor. From his analysis, it can be said that poverty is a choice, and there are many things to do to maintain poverty, just as there are many things to do to be successful.

The economic conditions of Black people in the Motherland and around the world are unacceptable. It seems as if Black people represent poverty and need, whereas other people are known for their riches and greatness. This conception can only be changed when Black people understand that their condition is not caused by anyone but themselves.

As a Black man, it was hard for me to accept the fact that I was responsible for my own conditions because I had always believed that someone else was responsible for my situation. I believed that I was not productive because somebody did not want me to be and I lived in a shattered house and environment because I was not given what I merited. I thought I was treated unfairly because of the color of my skin. It is possible that many feel the same in the modern-day world as I felt previously.

Careful observation of the comportments, behaviors, attitudes, vision, characters and reasoning of some Black people made me understand why certain things have gone the way they have. No matter the excuses any Black man would give concerning their economic or social status, the Black man must know that he is the captain of his own ship and he is responsible for how it sails.

Some years back, I spoke to an African man who refused to secure a job, not because he was not qualified, but because he intentionally refused to work. I asked him what his problem was, and he boldly replied that he did not come to Europe to work but to take what belonged to his ancestors. He explained that the Europeans came to Africa to steal their goods some years back and he had come also to steal to take back to Africa. He told me on a serious note that he would only steal because he could not work for any White man.

Many young African girls walking on the streets in Europe are prostituting themselves for money because they must pay their sponsors huge amounts, because their own African brothers and sisters, who promised to bring them to Europe for better opportunities, later forced them into the business of prostitution. Some of these girls said to me, they knew they were coming to Europe to be prostitutes, but they had no choice because life was difficult in Africa and coming to Europe to prostitute themselves was the only chance they had to improve their economic status. I disagree with them because prostitution is not the only option in life.

Young boys from Africa, who also made their way to Europe, go about begging for money, stealing and some are selling drugs, as if these are the only things Black people could do. The disgraceful comportments some Black people put up sometimes make me truly sad.

I have had the opportunity to interact with many Black people because of my position as a leader in the Black community and I have seen and heard things that marveled me tremendously.

I once asked a Black lady who came to me for counsel what she wanted to do in life and she replied and said, "I want to marry and give birth to my children before people think that I am barren". I asked her if that was all she wanted in life. I also explained that perhaps educating herself and earning herself some degree could put her in good stead for getting a job which could help her when she got married. She explained that as a Black woman, she had to have all her children early and that she did not need a job for that, because God would provide for her and her children.

In one of his programs, the Ghanaian TV presenter, Nana Ansah Kwao dealt with an interesting topic where he exposed the new trend in Ghana and some African countries concerning **Gold in the Gulf**. In this program, he told the audience how African men and women lure their own young African brothers and sisters into believing that there are job opportunities awaiting them in some Asian countries which are better than what they have in their own countries. These young people follow their African brothers' and sisters' enticing offers to later find out that it was nothing other than slavery. They sell their own people for money. They do not care about the consequences of their betrayal which, most times, includes the suffering of their own brothers and sisters in a foreign land. These slave-sellers are only concerned with the temporal gain.

The problem here is not the White man or the Westerners; these are Africans selling their own brothers and sisters, in this 21st Century, into slavery for money. Some are sold into prostitution, which is now a big African business, some turn whole communities into drug markets, some are known for internet fraud and some for stealing. Kidnapping of people to ransom for money has also become a lucrative job.

One of my colleagues visited his country in Africa and had the shock of his life. He said to me, "I was in a taxi with a young man, estimated to be about 23 years old, who was making some frustrating sounds in the car, so I asked him, 'young man, what is your problem?' He said, "I am so frustrated because I don't have money like other people. I don't have a house of my own, cars and women as I would want to; life is so hard for me and I am ready to do anything to get money, even to the extent of killing my mother for ritual money". My colleague said his bones chilled on hearing what this 23-year-old young man had to say about his own mother.

After using his potential and abilities to do these things, the Black man then turns back to say he does all these things because he is a victim of racism, injustice and unfairness, using his color and his pattern of thought as an excuse. There are no excuses for the Black man, either in the Motherland or anywhere he dwells, because there is nothing wrong with him except the choice he makes to express his pattern of thoughts.

Armed robbery is now the "JOB" that has employed thousands of young Africans who go about, sometimes in the day and mostly in the night, armed more than the local police themselves, breaking into homes and stealing at gun-point, most times killing their victims in cold blood. Men now kill for telephones, TVs, cars, money and the like. They invade the homes of Black people just like them who have worked hard to achieve some comfort in life, and, at gun-point, steal all their belongings.

A man I know told me of an experience he had with thieves as he returned from work. He said that he saw 8 men approach him in a corner demanding his phone and wallet. As he said no, they all jumped on him and beat him mercilessly. They took his wallet and telephone and wristwatch and wanted to kill him because he did not surrender immediately just as they wanted. He survived with severe injuries with his life barely spared.

After making our own countries look like hell, we, the Black people, now look for other good grounds abroad to exhibit our behaviors and comportments and when we are confronted, we turn it into a racial situation. It cannot be denied that the way some issues have been handled by the police authorities in some parts of Europe, and most especially in the United States of America (USA), are incorrect and inappropriate. There is true evidence of hate and racism in the handling of some of the arrests and control by the police in the USA and other Western countries. However, it must also be noted that the wrong committed by a few White people cannot be used to judge all White men. The behaviors of the police are no excuse to deter Black people from rising above limitations. These behaviors should rather invoke Black people to seek higher education to be able to occupy certain positions that would permit them to change certain laws that would benefit all people.

On January 20th of 2009, Barack Hussein Obama, an American with African roots, ascended to the seat of government as the President of the USA. His presidency was not only significant for the American people, but it gave hope to all Black people in the world. No one thought that something of that nature would ever happen, but President Barack Hussein Obama made it clear to all Black people, whether African Americans, African Africans, African Asians, African Europeans, African Australians or Africans on other planets, that none of them have any excuse.

President Barack Hussein Obama led America successfully in his first and second terms in office and handed over power to his successor. He did not become President because he was a tall and handsome man, nor did he become President because his mother was a White woman. Importantly, he did not become President because he was favored by the American people, especially as he was not the first man whose father was Black and mother White. He became the President because he studied and prepared himself over the years through hard work, determination, discipline and sacrifices. President Obama studied and pursued his dreams. He addressed all limitations and strove for the highest office and he won. He did not allow anything to stop him because he knew that he had all it took to lead the nation.

There are no valid excuses for any Black man on earth, no matter where they are born, because the principles for poverty and success operate when and wherever they are applied. There are successful Black people in every field of operation who are doing great things. Black inventors, Black business men and women, Black lawyers, doctors, pilots, engineers, architects, actors, entertainers, sportsmen, professors, and so on, who have demonstrated their abilities and contributed to enhancing the lives of humanity. The majority of Black people have not understood that they are the cause of their own failures and inability to arise.

"The Black man has no excuses, and must not make excuses"

CHAPTER TWENTY

The Necessity of Unity

United we stand and divided we fall is a sacrosanct truth, the consequence of which, when applied, is overwhelming. When people put their forces together, they become unstoppable. A single bee is not a threat to a man, but ten bees can sabotage a man's strength and cause him to run.

What has helped a lot of businesses and organizations, families, societies and nations is unity. People unite to put their strength together to achieve greater performances. Though, single-handedly, some people can achieve progress, uniting individual forces results in greater and better output.

Though the lion is big and strong, most times, they work as a team (pride) to catch their prey. They unite their forces and hunting skills to provide for their families, saving time and energy. One lion could be overpowered by a bigger animal, but a pride of lions is an armed force.

America is great because of its United States. America is a super-power nation, and there is no controversy about that. Anything about the United States of America is great and attractive. It is true that every republic has a President, but the President of the USA represents superior power.

Individual European countries, though strong economically and socially, saw the need to unite their forces to increase their strength as one nation. Europe is very great now because they have one currency, one common market and one vision. They work hard to improve their union to benefit the citizens.

One thing very common about the Chinese people is how they group themselves in any nation they migrate to and how they promote their businesses. They might have their own shortcomings but at least they work together.

One of the secrets for survival is to learn how to work together as a team, protecting one another and caring for one another. When people come together, they benefit from their human resources such as knowledge, skills, abilities and potential. They also benefit from their natural resources to strengthen themselves economically and socially.

When two millionaires, each having 750 million dollars, unite their money, they are no longer referred to as millionaires but rather billionaires because they had the sense to unite their money to have more strength to make bigger investments that could procure greater profit.

Unity is strength, it is power, and it gives authority. Unity is a great advantage. Those who understood the benefit of unity have become richer and stronger. It is a true saying that whoever works alone, dies alone, and an army is always better than a single fighter. It is only in Hollywood that one fighter can destroy a whole nation. However, life is not a movie.

Even when bad people unite, their evil is great, so how much more when good people unite? A weak man in an army is covered because the strength of others protects him from the enemy and the boldness of others covers his weaknesses. There are nations that understood the power of unity and as they united under one flag, they benefited and did incredible things that shocked the world. I have never been to Japan, but I love the Japanese for their unity, hard work and determination. They are a very strong nation because they are united.

When it comes to Africans, or Black people in general, it is a different story. It is like Africans, or the Black man, is oblivious to the benefits of unity. It is not clear what has caused Africans or Black people not to unite. Black people are the ones who need to unite more than any group of people on earth because of their story. One of the major factors that has restricted the progress and development of the African is disunity.

As a continent, rich with all kinds of resources, Africa does not reflect her wealth in her people. However, other people who have united their forces, and none of African origin, have taken control of Africa's wealth and they now determine how it must be sold and the conditions of payment.

The African nations know very well that they must unite their forces just like others have done but they have reluctantly played around this vital decision, loosing every little power and control they have over transactions and decisions regarding export and import. The disunity among the African nations has gone a long way to affect the African people by separating them and making them behave like enemies.

In the Diaspora, unity of Black people is still a great problem. Blacks kill Blacks and betray one another. They take advantage of one another and destroy themselves. Black gangs from one area fight other Black gangs from another area. Deadly shootings and innumerable premature deaths among young Black folks occur because of hatred and offenses birthed by disunity.

There are so many things going on among Black people in Africa that are not told and many of these issues do not make sense. An example is how a man killed and cut off the head of his nephew as a ritual for money because there is a belief that when you sacrifice a human being unto certain shrines, the gods will let you have money for a certain period before dying. This basically means selling of one's soul to the devil and many people have indulged in such awful and inhumane acts by killing innocent people for money. When a people are not united, they do not see their value; neither do they see the value of their own people.

Tribal differences separate Black people from the same nation and cause division among the same people. Dialectal differences cause problems which ought not to be so. The Rwandan civil war that occurred in 1994 could have been avoided if the people had seen themselves as one. Some Black people hate other Black people because they see them as different.

I wonder why Black people accuse the White people of racism if they practice racism to the highest level against their own brothers. When one interacts with Africans from different nations, that is where Black racism is discovered. Black people condemn one another and segregate from one another. They prefer to do it alone instead of reasoning among themselves to benefit from each other's abilities and potential.

If Europeans have united because they have seen the benefit of it, then Black people must put away their differences and unite as well and this unity must be engaged in immediately. The development of Africans or Black people depends on their ability to unite as one people.

So many Black people have died in the USA, killed by their own brothers based on irrelevant issues. Africans kill Africans and then complain of racism from White people. The highest crime is to take a life. Killing someone because you do not feel that they merit being alive is the highest level of racism.

Disunity has made Black people vulnerable. It is hard, most times, to trust a Black brother because he will betray you when you least expect it. Most Black people prefer to unite with other people than to unite with Black folks to create or do something together because they are able to work with a clearer mind with others than with their own people.

It appears that Black people do not understand the power of unity and the Black man does not realize that his progress, his strength, his wisdom and skills, his happiness and great achievements depend on the ability to unite with others. Until the Black man is capable of overcoming isolation and individualism, he will continue to be used by others to achieve their purpose. The survival and the progress of Africa depend on her unification and the earlier she does this, the better it would be for her people.

The reggae king, Bob Marley, dedicated a song to this scope telling Africans in his song, **Africa Unite**. He urged Africans to see the importance of their unification and he urged them to come together and make it work. However, Black people have not risen to the call for unity.

I thought the disunity of the African nations was due to the language barrier, but the Europeans do not speak the same language, yet they are united. Black people must not be blind to this vital subject but must work hard to promote its realization.

"Black people must unite"

CHAPTER TWENTY-ONE

The Past, A Resevoir of Information

Everybody has a past in which sometimes some things they remember make them proud and some things do not, and they wished some things never happened. The past can either cripple you or push you, depending on how you saw and understood it, the lessons you learnt from it, and how you implemented those lessons.

Sometimes, a person can refuse to do anything to improve themselves because of certain evil things that happened to them. They may allow what happened to them to halt their progress whereas other people may decide not to allow this to distort their progress or give satisfaction to those negative or brutal things that happened to them. Instead, they may use the pains that they went through to propel them to work hard to achieve great success. It is true that the past could be painful, but how it is used is very important.

Once, a footballer was asked, "Why are you so determined on the field and why do you put all your strength into scoring a goal"? and he responded, "when I remember the suffering, the poverty and the hardship my mother went through to put food on the table for me and my brothers and sisters to eat, I take no chances because I want poverty not to come near my family, therefore, anytime I'm on the field, I remember myself, where I'm coming from and I do what I must do by turning my pain to success".

Until we understand that even the negative things we experience in life are for a purpose, the past will always have power and control over us. A person who carefully observes their past understands how to use the power and control of their past to build their future, in other words, turning their pain into their strength.

In the years 1939-1945, Germany went through a horrible devastating condition, where the Nazi regime, under Adolf Hitler, killed a lot of people and ended up destroying the country as well. Germany learnt a hard lesson and has not engaged itself in any war after the Second World War. Nevertheless, they did not allow their past to sabotage and dominate their country. Rather, they pulled through and worked hard to rebuild their country, making it even better than it was before it was destroyed. Germany is one of the most advanced and strongest nations in the world.

History tells of how many kingdoms, nations and families have experienced disasters that should have terminated their existence but surprisingly, they pulled themselves together and fought to become better. They vowed never to allow their past to hold them down by fortifying their success with vigor.

It takes a mature person to recognize the importance of the past to understand better how to live in the future. The lazy person only sees the pains of the past as an opportunity to fold their hands and complain, looking for every excuse to justify themselves. Their past becomes their bed; it becomes their life and an excuse for not improving themselves.

Scientist continuously research the past to understand the present world and to understand what to do or expect in the future. Most of the discoveries they make from their research of the past enable them to solve certain mysteries in today's world. They see the past as a reservoir of information.

The Black man has a bitter past. Unfortunately, most of his stories have been twisted and some remain untold. He learnt some bad things about himself which have conditioned him, but, through the hard work of many Black scholars, the true image, identity and history of the Black man has been revealed. No matter how long it was concealed and misinterpreted, the Black man now knows who he is.

Unfortunately, the Black man has allowed his past to ensnare him. He has permitted his past to condition his present and future and this has sabotaged his performance. Many people are expecting to see developments and the control of wealth and affairs from the Black man because his past is full of rich history which should propel him towards great achievements. However, the opposite is what is seen.

Instead of turning his pain into gain, he has used his pain as an excuse. Instead of using his rich history to work hard into greatness, he always uses his condition to beg for help. Therefore, most of the evil things written about him continue to fight him. Many people still believe the lies that are written and spoken about the Black man because he has refused to turn his past into his strength.

The Black people have paid dearly to live on that land. The evil that was designed against them destroyed their progress for a long time. The painful history of the Black people has the power to either cease their functionality or propel them into becoming great people. Some of the stories of the sufferings of the Black people who were sold into slavery are so inhumane that it brings fresh memories whenever it is told. These pains have the power to cause a halt in the mind of the Black man, because it hurts him badly, and unfortunately, there are still incidents that are happening presently that are reviving the sores.

For example, until the Black people in the United States are able to turns their pains into their strength, they will always be victims. Their pain must make them be determined to take education seriously. They must understand that they cannot continue to fight on the streets with stones and sticks but must educate themselves to occupy positions of authority in the land. In the government, there must be millions of them, in the police and military, scholars and scientists, businesses and wealth, in every arena where decisions are made, the Black man must make sure that innumerable numbers of them are there to influence decisions that are made that do not favor them. It took the Black people there too long to get one Black President because of how they were labeled. A Black President should have happened long before it did.

President Barrack Obama's success as President was not to promote Black pride but to give hope to all Black people in the United States and to tell them that the United States is their land too, and they must turn their pain into their strength by taking advantage of the present system and structures made available to all its citizens.

Instead of the numerous complaints, accusations, fights and personal revenges, education is the key.

The Black people in America must understand that the US is not made up of only Black people. Thus, if they refuse to educate themselves and enter the system that determines and makes decisions on how the nation must run, then they must not lament if laws and decisions are made that do not favor them. Those who make laws are more powerful than those who break them. The law, although it can be manipulated by wealth, also punishes the wealthy. For this reason, all must abide by laws set, whether poor or rich.

There must be millions of Barrack Obamas in the USA and they must all rise. The more there are Black Presidents and Black people in authority, the more the injustices, partiality and racism would disappear. However, if Black people continue to use their pain as an excuse not to educate themselves and not to progress, and if the Black man continues to depend on benefits and government subsidiaries, then his latter condition will be worse than his former.

The Africans in the Motherland are expected to do double, because they rule themselves and make decisions on their own. Unlike those in the United States and those in other parts of the world, the Africans in the Motherland rule themselves and are supposed to use all their strength to develop themselves, but this has not been the case. The numbers of Africans who are leaving the continent for Western countries of late are alarming and a great shame. It is saddening to think that the leaders of Africa arc not doing anything about this situation. They watch their youth leave the continent to become domestic workers abroad. Some turn into criminals, prostitutes and beggars. The history of the Black people, which should have provoked them to educate themselves to build their nations, has conditioned them negatively thus turning them into beggars and dependent people, always running for help and pleading to be rescued.

The pain women go through during childbirth is described as excessive. It would therefore be expected that women would refuse to get pregnant after the first experience of childbirth. However, this is not the case. Women continue to have children, some many more times than can be imagined. They do this because they know that the pain that they experience is nothing compared to the joy of having children. Therefore, they turn their pain into strength and forget about the undesirable situations they experience during pregnancy and birthing and they focus on what the outcome will be when the pain ends.

In the same way, Black people must consider history to know that they are not the only ones who have suffered in this unjust world. Many people have gone through horrible situations as well and those who allowed their pain to rule them became the servants of those who overcame and turned theirs into success. Black people need to focus on the joy they will experience if they can turn their pain into strength and into creativity.

I thought that coming from a poor home gave me the right to lament and complain because life had been unfair to me. When I saw rich people, I was angry because I thought they were privileged by divinity and were born into riches. This stopped the day I had the opportunity to work with an Italian man who owned a company. As we engaged in conversation, he explained that when he was young, his parents were very poor. He was the third of eight brothers and sisters.

He explained that he did not go to high school because there was no money. They had to wake up early in the morning, around 3:00 am, to walk 20 miles to a farm and work. They walked for hours to get to the farm and worked just to have enough money to buy some food to eat. They worked very hard to save some money to start a family business which he developed, hence the company. He explained that life is not that easy for everyone but hard work and determination with planning always yield good fruit. His eyes were full of tears as he told me of how he lost some of his brothers due to the hard life.

He advised me not to allow my past to hinder my future but to turn my pain into strength. He went on to explain the importance of ignoring his present state but acknowledging where he has come from. His pain gave him the strength to fight for the best.

I have since pondered on our conversation. On reflection, I realized that my youth was better than this man's youth as I did not experience some of the horrors he experienced. Therefore, if he overcame his pain and strove for success, what stops me from striving even more and what stops me from turning my pain into strength? I learnt a great lesson which was that I had **NO EXCUSE**.

"The Black man must turn his pain into his strength".

CHAPTER TWENTY-TWO

Change, Love and Character-Building

Sometimes, when we are faced with the truth, we react negatively to it because truth is bitter though it saves lives. Deception is sweet, but it destroys everything when the truth is revealed. Unfortunately, many people do not want to know the truth. In the Holy Bible, it is written that,

'You will know the truth and the truth shall make you free'.

This concerns every situation in life.

You cannot know if you do not dedicate time to study by observing, analyzing, experimenting and implementing and when you discover the truth by observing, experimenting or analyzing, then you must be willing to accept it. To the best of my knowledge, life is a mystery and those who research about life discover new things every day.

One fact that many will agree with is that there is not much love in the world. The lack of love and the hatred displayed by many was what resulted, and continues to result, in slavery and control. Humans tend not to love each other.

Even animals respect each other, and they know that the earth does not belong to just one group of animals but that the many distinct species in every group beautifies and contributes to form the animal kingdom.

When it comes to love, humans are very disappointing. We have fought and killed and destroyed one another and we continue to do so. We have developed weapons of mass destruction to kill ourselves on this planet. We talk about peace, but we are not at peace. We know about the power of love, but we practice evil and hatred. We know what the solution is, but we only create trouble and we are worried about planet Earth becoming unstable, but we continue to do things to make it more unstable, thus, worsening the situation.

One generation passes, and another rises to intensify the evil. All the people we classify as great caused pain and sorrow, yet they had the opportunity and resources to rectify things and make the world better. It is not all doom and gloom since we can testify that some people who worked hard to contribute to the suffering of humanity are now dead and buried. The only worrying aspect is that although we can testify to this, we continue to busy ourselves devising sophisticated weapons to destroy one another.

Black people have many things to put in place as far as their lives are concerned. They need to accept responsibility and work hard to improve their living. A higher percentage of Black people are still suffering as compared to those who have broken the limitations. The work to perform is still great especially as most Black people have not understood their value.

There is this common belief among Black people that they are cursed and that is why their color is different from everyone else's. Some of the early biblical teachings in the church were not favorable to the Black man because Black men were made to think that they were the descendants of Cain who was cursed by God. This generalized belief occurred because most Black people only believed what they heard rather than studying for themselves. Apostle Paul in the Bible told Timothy to study to show himself approved unto God (2 Timothy 2:15). God has not cursed Black people and they are not the descendants of Cain.

Some of the books that were written against the Black man to degrade him and cause him to believe that he was not a human being but a slave and inferior to other groups of people were just to psychologically distort his thinking and arrest his functionality and productivity. The teachings by these professors and so-called intellectuals were aimed at promoting White supremacy and because the power and authority were bent in that direction, their hypotheses and wrong theories were endorsed, accepted and approved for public education.

That is why the Black man must take education seriously. In Africa or abroad, the Black man has a poor self-image which makes him think and operate in a different way, causing severe problems in his life.

Education is important, but wrong education is poisonous. It is, therefore, an obligation for a person to acquire the right education to stimulate the brain to think and analyze truths pertaining to life. One of the greatest tragedies in life is to believe something that is wrong for a long time and live by it.

In the medical field, many doctors have committed errors during surgical operations on their patients. Some accidentally left tools in the bodies of their patients and closed the flesh (See ThoughtCo.com for objects commonly left inside patients after surgery). The patient lived with this tool inside them complaining of pains for years, until it was discovered. The patients complained of pain continuously, but the doctor's response was always, "It is a psychological pain". After further analysis, the doctors were shocked to discover that the pains of the patient were due to the doctor's mistake. If the patients had not insisted, they would have died prematurely because someone did a wrong thing and told them that they had to adapt to the pain because it was psychological.

Most Black people have adapted to a certain lifestyle because they think they are cursed by God and that they are inferior to other people. There are some White people going about speaking boldly that the Black man is inferior to the White man and many other similar misconceptions and idiocy, and unfortunately, most Black people have believed them.

Certain things and thoughts can condition the life of a person but that does not mean that they are inferior in thinking. The thoughts that have been left in the brain and soul of the Black man must be taken seriously and be removed otherwise he will have to live by them forever.

The only person who can remove the stronghold in the minds of the Black man is himself. The Black man must assume the responsibility for educating his people rightly to eliminate the conception he has about himself and change his own thoughts.

There are too many uneducated Black people handling the issues of the Black man wrongly. Instead of education, they use rebellion, instead of reasoning, they use fighting and the more they use these primitive methods, the more they prove others right about them. Most Black people have rejected education because they think it belongs to the White man, which is wrong because knowledge gives power and illiteracy gives servitude. Therefore, those who have knowledge rule over those who do not.

The way the Children of the Black Man have handled the sacrifices their fathers made to obtain some amount of dignity and to enable their freedom is very bad. The price the Fathers paid and the difficulties they encountered just to ensure the next generations matched up to, and reached above standards, was enormous, but this price is not reflected in the actions of this generation of Black people.

Dr. Martin Luther King Jr., said,

"I have a dream that one day my four little children will one day live in a nation where they will not be judged by the color of their skin but by the content of their character".

Dr Martin Luther King made it clear in his speech that his children, referring to all Black people, would not be judged by their skin color but by the **CONTENT** of their **CHARACTER**.

Merriam Webster Dictionary defines Character as,

"The way someone thinks feels and behaves, someone's personality, a set of qualities that are shared by many people in a group, country"

OR,

"A set of qualities that makes a place or thing different from other places or things".

Considering these definitions, Dr Martin Luther King Jr. implied that it was wrong to judge, hinder, deny, deprive and segregate a man because of his color instead of the way he thinks, feels and behaves, which represents his true personality. His fight was to make every human being see the truth about the human race, to promote that we are equal no matter our skin color.

According to Merriam Webster dictionary, the personality of a man defines his character which agrees with what Dr Martin Luther King also said. Therefore, the way a person thinks or behaves or feels in the society is very important. This is to say that if a person could be identified by the way he thinks, behaves and feels, then a people can also be identified by their character.

Just as every individual has his own character, every group of people also has their character, something that represents that group of people, which basically could be changed depending on their own desires and how their character affects or promotes their lives.

Most Black people must work greatly on their character, because the content of their character is procuring more troubles for them and hindering their own progress. Though there are some Black people who have developed their personalities to attain greatness, the majority of Black people are faced with character issues.

Education is the method used to correct character because every child born needs to be educated to correct certain behaviours before it forms part of their personality. A baby cries at any time when he or she wants something; the baby excretes without any warning; the baby vomits when he or she has had enough food and continues to make noise as a way of expressing himself or herself instead of talking. A baby soon learns that these behaviours are inappropriate, and, as he or she grows, they learn other more civil ways to express themselves. Thus, through education, the baby is corrected on how to comport and express themselves, but if the baby is left unchecked and continues to behave that way, even as an adult, then the baby's situation becomes noticeable by all people. Nelson Mandela said that,

"Education is the powerful weapon which you can use to change the world".

The conception people have about the Black man is not only about his color, but about the way he thinks and behaves. Unfortunately, there is a pattern of thought and certain behaviours commonly seen among Black people that must be checked and stopped.

Whether or not it is connected to slavery or colonialism, the character of the Black man must be checked, admitted and changed. The whole educational system of the Black man must be analysed and corrected before it damages and marks all the generations to come. Affirmatively, it is not only the Black man who has problems with character, but the Black man has permitted certain things to differentiate him so much from other people which has made most people to think that he is inferior as a human being. It cannot be denied that the Black man has demonstrated in everything that he thinks and functions like everyone else except in the illiteracy and wrong education that has crippled many.

The future of the Children of the Black Man is still uncertain because millions of young Africans who have abandoned education are migrating without control to Europe and other parts of the world to look for money and most of them do not even see the need to continue their education. Many exchange the opportunity for education with donkey jobs just to survive.

The character of the Black man is not the responsibility of the government in the countries they migrate to. They are only taught to obey the laws of the country if permitted to enter and are told the consequences of breaking the law. Sadly, most Black men end up having problems with the law because of their character and are jailed as criminals.

Most Black people are considered as criminals or as trouble-makers. Therefore, they are monitored wherever they go. The color 'Black' cannot be hidden among other people, so it makes identification and accusation very easy. Unfortunately, most Black people always want to outsmart the law by involving themselves in things forbidden by the law, so they are arrested, accused and jailed. Therefore, it has been concluded that Black people are criminals and aggressive and undisciplined trouble-makers and must be monitored, whether single or as a group.

The Children of the Black Man have not understood the value of life and the necessity of education. They reject education and follow their own childish thinking claiming that nobody could teach them anything. They form gangs and groups and devise unskilful ideas to express their convictions until they are surprised and arrested by the authorities and jailed for years. Sometimes, it is sad to see a Black man jailed for 20 years or more for a crime that makes no sense.

Their lives are wasted, and, kept behind bars, their characters worsen and their personality is damaged. Black people have still not understood this old **Tom** and **Jerry** game played on them and they fall victim all the time.

There are nations like Japan, South Korea and Germany that had to change their way of thinking to develop their countries to favour their citizens. We read about the Second World War where Germany played a pivotal role. They destroyed their own country and caused so many atrocities because of a wrong way of thinking. A bad pattern of thought turned a people to be aggressive towards everyone and made them engineer a war that made no sense, destroying lives and halting human progress. The wisdom of men was channelled to inventing and creating weapons of mass destruction to break down their own peace and prosperity.

No one thought that the Germans, after the Second World War, could rise to their present condition, but they have worked incredibly hard to rebuild their country and make their lives better. This level of achievement could only be attained when a people renew their minds and change their way of thinking through correct education by learning from past mistakes.

Japan and South Korea, and many other developed countries, adapted similar methods to improve their standard of living after understanding that wrong thinking can enslave a person or a people and keep them in bondage.

There is a level of thought that can break the grip of poverty on a person. When a person has nothing to offer, lack and poverty become their closest friends and all the advice they give to them leads to complicated troubles. The first method for dealing with lack and poverty is to change the way of thinking through proper education, and the second immediately follows and that is changing character.

There are nations that have suffered because of the way they thought and did things, but latterly understood that if they don't work hard on their way of thinking and change certain comportments, their situation could be permanent, and their condition would keep on worsening. They decided to achieve this through the vehicle of change, which is education.

Instead of change, the Children of the Black Man are adapting to their condition and making unpardonable errors. Very little emphasis is placed on the education that brings reformation.

If all the youth are running away from the Motherland to Europe, the USA and other parts, not to attend school but just to clean people's houses and work in the factories as labourers for very little pay, then the future of Africa or the Black people is at great risk. What this means is that Black people are still the labour force and have not reached the level of decision-making.

The progress of Africa must not be based on some few individuals or some few buildings built in the capital cities to beautify an area like we see in Europe. The progress of Africa must be looked at from a wider perspective considering the standard of life of the entire people. Africans are still suffering greatly, and it is a shame for all Black people, especially those who are chosen as leaders to rule the countries.

One thing I have observed in the Western countries is that leaders who loved their people and their country sacrificed and fought for the progress of the people by putting certain things in place that would help the development of their country. They did not take the country's resources to deposit in Africa and send their families to hide in some African nations so that when they are no longer in power, they would have access to that wealth as personal benefits while their country suffers. This is precisely what happens in Africa.

The news2.onlinenigeria.com confirms the list released of some 25 Nigerian politicians who have looted the country's money and deposited it in the USA and some few European banks as personal wealth. While Nigeria is going through a serious economic disaster, the very leaders who were supposed to craft a plan to save the country are the ones extracting the economic strength and perverting the road to save the nation.

These are the very few that have been exposed. What about the monies hidden in the other European nations and other parts of the world? What wealth has been hidden in other parts of the world which are untold? It is unfortunate that only Nigerian politicians were exposed, but the truth is that other African leaders are also culprits. This behaviour makes the Western people think that Black people have serious psychological issues. All the monies that African leaders have deposited in the Western banks has helped the Europeans to develop their countries without much stress. Probably, there are even monies deposited for which the owners could no longer be traced because it was done secretly by an individual.

How many Westerners have ever stolen their country's money and deposited it in any African bank? Or have moved their families to stay in any African nation to escape political attacks? Yet, thousands of corrupt African leaders, who were voted by their own people to help their nations, took that as an opportunity to loot the country's resources and deposit them in Europe to help the already advanced countries enjoy a wealth they did not work for while the poor African nations that need help are kept in the pit of poverty.

This is where I have a big problem when the White man is used as an excuse for the condition of Africa or Black people. I believe that we have a mind of our own and we are responsible for using our own mind. We do what we believe is the best for us, therefore, we must also be ready to take responsibility for our own thoughts and actions.

Africans, or Black people in general, must stop the victim syndrome and they must see their condition of today as self-afflicted.

My heart cries for the millions of children born in Africa who will eventually pay for the wickedness of selfish people who could have changed their generation to favour the incoming ones.

The children of the Black man are disappointing the fathers on a great scale. The children have chosen to be idle and not to use their resources to improve their lives. They prefer to play and have taken life as a game because they think their fathers have paid enough for their lives and that their role is to enjoy and do whatever they like. Whilst others are seriously advancing, the children of the Black man are moving from country to country seeking for domestic jobs to make a living. The children of the Black man must know that their condition is self-made and that they are the only ones who can change their situation. The great leader, Nelson Mandela said,

"Poverty is not an accident. Like slavery and apartheid, it is man-made and can be removed by the actions of man".

Let us learn to love one another. The Black man must change his character and must do so by educating himself whilst working hard and applying all the principles of success and love to better himself.

"The Progress of the Children of the Black Man depends on Love, Unity and a Change of Character".

www.ingramcontent.com/pod-product-compliance
Lightning Source LLC
Chambersburg PA
CBHW050726030426
42336CB00012B/1434